Christmas
with
Southern Living®
1981

Compiled & Edited by Candace N. Conard and Jo Voce

Oxmoor House, Inc. Birmingham

ISBN: 0-8487-0522-X
Manufactured in the United States of America
First Printing

Title page: The most meaningful gift is something you have made yourself. These gifts are fun to make, to give, and to eat: (clockwise from top left) Filled Christmas Cookies (page 86), Toasted Pecans (page 96), Hot Mocha Mix (page 62), Filled Christmas Cookies, Candied Fresh Coconut (page 81), Bourbon Pralines (page 80), Cranberry Jelly (page 92), Honey Nut Loaves (page 63), Holiday Relish (page 93), Homemade Curry Powder (page 98), Cream Cheese Braids (page 64), and Old-Fashioned Christmas Cookies (page 87).

Contents

The Joys of Giving 99

Christmas around the South 113

Christmas Journal 123

Contributors 140

Introduction

hristmas with Southern Living is for Southerners, those giving, loving people who know that the only way to keep the spirit of Christmas is to share it. Southern Christmases are full of the same abundance and joy as celebrations in other parts of the country but for many Southerners, the Christmas season is filled with family traditions and promises that are uniquely ours.

Each chapter of this book is a surprise package filled with the special pleasures of Christmas—all designed to help you enjoy the hustle and bustle of your preparations and to fill this holiday with excitement, joy, and imagination.

"Decorating for the Holidays" offers fresh suggestions and how-tos for drawing the bright colors and sparkle of Christmas throughout your home, including unexpected ways to trim the tree. "Christmas Bazaar"—an exciting variety of imaginative holiday ornaments and crafts to make together

and then to share. "Celebrations from the Kitchen"—tantalizing promises of aromas from the kitchen with tempting new recipes to enhance the holiday banquet. "Joys of Giving"— bright ideas and sources for exceptional new gifts and new ways to give them. "Christmas around the South"—the best of the season's happenings in each of the Southern states, complete with dates, times, and contacts. And "Christmas Journal"—to help plan and preserve this best of all Christmases.

This is the season when each of us delights in sharing activities that give our celebration of Christmas its own unique spirit. It is our hope that the ideas packed within these pages will both enhance the holiday traditions that your family already treasures and add new traditions that you will enjoy for years to come. But we hope, too, that you will share with us your holiday pleasures and expectations of Christmas with Southern Living so that future issues will continue to reflect your ideas of how best to celebrate the magic of the season.

Decorating for the Holidays

Many of our early thoughts about the Christmas holidays revolve around how we'll decorate our home. Long-treasured symbols of past family holidays, hidden safely in tissue paper for 11 months, are now lovingly brought down from the attic to once more add glitter and excitement to our homes. But even if we decorate with these favored and preserved ornaments, we are always interested in new ideas to add enthusiasm to the family gathering—a different way to display the candlesticks, or a show-stopping centerpiece, or a dramatic new door arrangement.

"Decorating for the Holidays" is a mélange of wonderful ideas for festooning your home both indoors and out, including a look at how neighbors decorate together. Basic instructions for making all the recognizable and expected holiday embellishments such as foliage clusters, wreaths, and garlands are given. But the most unexpected decorating ideas are here for you to make as well. Dried artichoke accents for a thick garland, a vine wreath wrapped in gold, a pyramid of osage oranges, a luscious red cranberry wreath, baskets made of pine cones and nuts, delicate snowflakes made simply from Queen Anne's lace blossoms—and ribbons everywhere.

A portion of this chapter is devoted entirely to Christmas trees, beginning with guidelines to help you choose a tree well suited to your needs. Three distinctive "specialty" trees are featured—one for shell collectors, one with ornaments inspired by nature, and a live tree festooned with fruit—complete with instructions for making the ornaments should you wish to try a new look this year.

Few of the ideas in this chapter are expensive; all are easy to duplicate. "Decorating for the Holidays" is devoted to making the most of this season of abundance by using the profusions of reds and greens, silvers and golds, candles and greenery to create in your home the magic that is Christmas.

Spruce up the Outside

Neighborhood Celebrations

Christmas brings out the best in people. Relatives, neighbors, business associates, and friends all reach out to each other to revel in the essence of the Christmas season.

Whole communities throughout the South make Christmas a time to share ideas and excitement and to celebrate the holidays together. Activities often become traditions, carried out for years by each addition to the community. Many such celebrations include block parties, open-house receptions, roving groups of carolers, cookie "swaps," visits from Santa Claus, and snowmen competitions.

Two such neighborhood celebrations are shown on these pages. One, a quiet little circle of homes on Mountain Park Circle in Mountain Brook, Alabama, is decorated with tiny Christmas trees with colored lights for each front yard, and for a central grassy area there is a larger tree that features one glittering star. Bits of mirror reflect the lights a hundred fold, capturing for this cozy street the brightness and warmth of all Christmas thoughts.

The second community celebration shown here is actually a very merry holiday contest between neighbors on otherwise serene Brinkworth Street in Houston, Texas. Each neighbor erects his own version of "How Santa Comes to Town." The result is an incredible display of imagination and a major attraction for holiday sightseers.

Foliage Clusters

For this year's holiday door decoration, try a thick bouquet of greenery instead of the traditional wreath. The Southern garden offers a wealth of foliage for arranging into imaginative holiday decorations for doors, windows, mailboxes, fences, and gates—even lampposts. The arrangements can be as simple as a cluster of magnolia leaves tied with ribbon or as elaborate as several kinds of evergreen foliage intertwined with toys or ornaments.

The photographs shown on these pages offer an interesting array of foliage clusters from which to choose. Or design your own holiday cluster, personalizing it with accents or colors or shapes that interest you. The general instructions given below for selecting and assembling the greenery are applicable to any foliage arrangement.

When selecting greenery for a holiday cluster, keep in mind that most evergreens with thick-leaved, waxy foliage will hold up well after cutting. Southern magnolia, Japan cleyera, rhododendron, holly, Japanese pittosporum, sweet olive, and loquat will last for several days without water; so will a number of short-needled evergreens, including hemlock, deodar cedar, and pines (Virginia, white, Scotch, and spruce). The foliage of some evergreens, such as rhododendron and Southern magnolia, will last for several weeks.

The cuttings of other evergreens such as gold-dust plant (aucuba), boxwood, mahonia, and yew will last longer when their stems are inserted in a block of florist's foam saturated with water. Just wire the foam into the base of the arrangement. For additional stem support, surround the florist's foam with chicken wire.

When pruning your evergreens for holiday decorations, be selective about where you make your cuts so that you do not destroy the shape of the plant.

Additional materials you will need for your foliage cluster are narrow-gauge florist's wire, a

Above: Welcome your holiday guests at the gate with a basket filled to overflowing with greenery, fruit, and berries. Florist's foam—or even a small jar of water—can sit inside the basket that is wired securely to the gate. This charming arrangement was created for the gardener's cottage in Colonial Williamsburg.

❧

Top: This foliage cluster adorning an outside windowsill accents the warmth of the candle and tree lights inside the house. Secure the pine cones and nandina berries to the cluster with florist's wire.

Right: Toys peeking out of a cluster of magnolia and pine become a whimsical door decoration that is especially appealing to youngsters.

A flat, woven basket used as a background provides contrast between the door and this arrangement of gold-dust plant (aucuba) and Japan cleyera. Lemons bring out the yellow in the variegated foliage.

Door decorations needn't be elaborate. They can be as simple as a cluster of shiny magnolia leaves tied with a bright red ribbon.

Bring your Christmas decorating talents all the way to the street with a mailbox dressed in greenery, pine cones, and bright red bows. Wire the foliage directly to the mailbox post.

roll of green florist's tape, U-shaped florist's pins, scissors, and a block of florist's foam if the greenery needs to be kept in water. For more interesting arrangements, you might collect various objects such as toys and ornaments to wire in with the foliage. Or, with the greenery, use natural materials such as fruit, pine cones, magnolia seed pods, and nuts. Dried foliage, such as eucalyptus, is also nice for creating contrast in color and texture.

For trim, you will need ribbons of various textures, widths, and patterns. If you want a background for the arrangement, consider using a flat basket, woven tray, or fan.

To assemble the foliage cluster (once you've decided on the shape), first choose several large branches to form the core of the arrangement. Use florist's tape and wire to hold the branches together, or insert the stems in a block of florist's foam and secure with tape and wire. Gradually add other pieces of greenery, wiring or pinning them in place as you develop the shape.

Wire in bows, toys, ornaments, or other objects as desired. You can also combine several types of foliage to provide interesting contrasts in color and texture.

If you are using a background such as a basket or fan for the door decoration, attach the completed foliage cluster to the background with florist's wire. When the arrangement is finished, use wire to hang it from a nail or from the door knocker.

Wreaths & Garlands

Christmas wreaths and garlands can be designed from many natural materials that are readily available. The basic greenery may come from conifers such as pines and junipers as well as other evergreens. Color may be added by using fruits such as apples or pomegranates or

For a truly "Southern" wreath, nestle cotton bolls, apples, holly berries, and wax myrtle against a thick background of common boxwood.

berries from holly, nandina, pyracantha, or chinaberries. Pine cones, nuts, sweet gum balls, and dried flowers of various sizes, shapes and textures—even small toys and ornaments, ribbons, or feathers—all add interest to your Christmas decorations.

A few basic guidelines are included here for working with greenery, fruits, berries, and pine cones and for making a basic greenery wreath and garland. The photographs in this section are all examples of these basic decorating techniques, but the choice of greenery and the addition of special "accents" makes each as individual as you wish your home to be when it is dressed up for the holidays.

To duplicate any of the ideas shown on these pages, simply work through the basic guidelines that follow; then check the captions for hints on what makes that particular wreath or garland so special. Separate instructions are given for a few of the more complicated or specialized decorating projects.

GREENERY

Careless pruning can ruin the shape of a tree and may kill a shrub. As a general rule, prune to shape. Make all cuts at a 45° angle and so that

The Arlington House wreath contrasts beautifully with the magnolia garlands. Pine cones, nuts, and pomegranate halves form an "inner" wreath framed by greenery for a striking welcome to all who visit this antebellum home.

ॐ

An impressive garland of shiny magnolia branches frames the doorway at historical Arlington House in Birmingham, Alabama. Although quite large, the weight of the garland may be easily supported by strategically placed hooks in the door frame. Smaller magnolia garlands are wired directly to the wrought-iron railings on either side of the door.

the finished cut will be hidden by the foliage that remains.

The key to making greens last inside your house is the conditioning you give them before you bring them indoors. Leave the greens in a bucket of water overnight in the garage or cool basement, but do not allow the water to freeze. They need this transitional period to absorb as much water as possible and to adjust to the change in temperature. You can facilitate the water absorption by lightly crushing the stem ends with a mallet or by splitting the ends with several 2"-long vertical cuts.

After conditioning overnight, holly, pine, and cedar stem ends should be dipped in candle wax to seal the resin. Even with this precaution, pine and cedar are not recommended for garlands because they can stain the walls. The wax will not aid in prolonging vase life.

Ivy will dry within a week out of water, but if you dip the ivy (stem, leaves, and all) into clear, liquid floor wax and let it dry overnight on newspaper, you can make the ivy appear lush for much longer.

The number of greens practical for decoration increases considerably if you can provide them with a continuous source of water. Florist's foam wrapped with chicken wire is a good base for arrangements of greenery because it not only holds the water supply, but it also acts as support for the stems.

Another hint to having your decorations last: when you "deck the halls," turn the thermostat down!

FRUITS & BERRIES

Fruits such as apples, pomegranates, and cranberries take on a wonderful holiday gloss from clear liquid floor wax, although it should be made clear to guests and family that the apples that look so inviting cannot be eaten. Vegetable oil is an edible gloss, but it should be used only where the oil will not get on clothes, linens, or upholstery.

Weight is the most important consideration when decorating with fruit, for it must be securely attached to wreaths and garlands. You may need to use both florist's wire and florist's picks to stabilize the fruit.

Push a piece of florist's wire crosswise through the center of the fruit and bring the ends down toward the base of the fruit. Twist these ends together (Diagram A) and wrap them around a wire wreath base or garland.

To secure fruit on a Styrofoam® or straw wreath base, or on a fruit pyramid with a soft base, you must use a florist's pick in conjunction with the wire going through the fruit. Make a hole in the base end of the fruit with the sharp end of the pick; then reverse the pick and push the blunt end into the fruit. Twist the ends of the cross wire tightly around the pick. (Diagram B.)

The plump clusters of nandina, pyracantha, and burford holly can be safely used in your holiday decorating if they are dipped in clear liquid floor wax, which helps to hold the berries on the stems. Dip clusters of berries and allow to dry overnight on newspaper. (You can reuse the wax many times.) The stems of berry clusters can be wired to florist's picks for more flexibility in arranging.

Rosehips, crab apples, sumac, and magnolia seedpods are also excellent possibilities for color that you may not have considered. Spray sumac and magnolia pods with inexpensive hair spray to keep the seeds intact.

PINE CONES

Their overlapping scales and subtle gray-to-brown coloring plus their myriad sizes and shapes make pine cones one of the most popular materials for holiday decorating. Nestled against a background of lush greenery, they provide the right touch of texture on many of the wreaths and garlands featured in this section.

To attach a pine cone to a garland or wreath of greenery, use precut lengths of 18- to 22-gauge florist's wire. Starting about ½" to 1" from the stem end of the cone, wrap the wire completely around the cone, pushing it between layers of

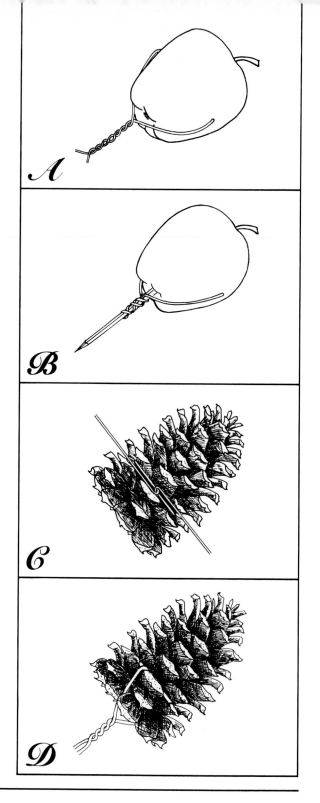

scales to conceal the wire. Cross the wire ends where they meet and backtrack with each end for a quarter of a circle until the ends are on opposite sides of the cone. (Diagram C.) Then pull the wire ends down to the stem end of the cone and twist the wires around each other. (Diagram D.) Wrap the ends of the wire around the wreath or garland to secure the cone in its place.

A *Using U-shaped florist's pins to secure the sprigs of greenery, completely cover the wreath base. Work around the base in one direction, covering the stems of each sprig with each additional bit of greenery. Fill in the inside and outside edges as you proceed.*

WREATHS

The base of a wreath may be a circle of wire, Styrofoam®, straw, or sphagnum moss wrapped tightly around a wire loop. For a more finished appearance, the straw and moss forms may be wrapped with strips of green or black plastic.

Always attach greenery to a wreath base so that each sprig lies in the same direction as it circles the form. For instance, start at the bottom of the form and work clockwise around the wreath so that each additional sprig of greenery conceals the stems of the previously attached sprig. Be sure to add greenery around the inside and outside circles of the base for a full, rounded wreath shape.

There are three different ways to attach greenery to a wreath, depending on the type of base you are using. For a straw or Styrofoam® base, the easiest way to secure the greenery is to pin each sprig in place with U-shaped florist's pins. This method is illustrated in the photographs on this page. A second method for securing greenery to a straw or Styrofoam® base is to tie several sprigs together around a florist's pick and then insert the pick into the base, always working around the circle in one direction.

B *To add color accents to your greenery wreath, follow the instructions for attaching wires to fruits and berries and to pine cones.*

For a sphagnum moss or rigid wire wreath base, each sprig of greenery must be wired onto the form. Use florist's wire and plenty of greenery for a thick, lush appearance.

GARLANDS

Boxwood and Japanese pittosporum are good choices for garlands, although pine can be used on a stair railing where it is not resting against a

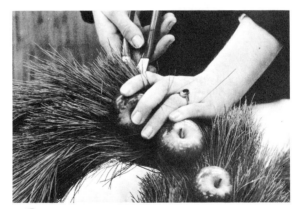

C *After securing all decorative material to the wreath, cut off excess wire from the back of the wreath with wirecutters.*

wall. The greenery should be tied into small, workable bunches.

Both boxwood and Japanese pittosporum require a rope support about ¼" thick. (If the rope is dyed green, it will take less greenery to conceal it.) Attach the greenery to the rope with a continuous roll of thin florist's wire. For a stair railing garland, start at one end of the rope, hold a cluster of greenery against the rope, and wrap wire around the stems, pulling it tightly against the rope. Continue wrapping wire around each subsequent cluster and the rope, always working in the same direction so that each additional cluster of greenery conceals the stems of the previously attached cluster.

For a garland that will be hung over a doorway or window, measure the length desired. Cut a piece of rope to this measurement and mark the center. Attach greenery to the rope with florist's wire in a wrapping motion as described above, but start in the *center* of the rope and work toward one end; then begin again in the center and work toward the opposite end. In this way, the greenery on the garland will fall in a uniform manner as it outlines the door or window.

Berries and pine cones or other bright accents may be wired into the garland as you are attaching the greenery. Follow the instructions under Fruits & Berries for wiring heavy fruits into a garland.

For a thicker pine garland without using rope, tie each cluster of greenery directly onto the preceding cluster. In this method, you are forced to tie the bunches of greenery close together, making a thick garland without gaps.

Ivy is a beautiful, natural garland—more delicate than pine—and requires no special preparation other than the conditioning described in the section on Greenery. Drape it loosely around door frames, chandeliers, and stair railings as the Victorians once did.

This handsome doorway features a thick garland of greenery accented with the spiky blossoms of dried artichokes. A wooden gable vent is a distinctive substitute for the traditional greenery wreath.

DRIED ARTICHOKE BLOSSOMS

MATERIALS:
   firm, unblemished artichokes
   tissue paper
   silica gel

Stuff pieces of tissue paper between the petals of each artichoke. Set the artichokes on their bases in a flat baking dish filled with 1" silica gel; the silica gel will absorb the moisture. Dry the artichokes in an oven set at less than 150° overnight or as long as 48 hours. (Drying time depends on the size of the artichokes.)

To vary the shapes of the blossoms, you may wish to force the petals of the artichokes into more open positions during the drying process.

The kitchen is often the hub of holiday activity, so don't neglect to add a wreath to the kitchen door to cheer the cook. Or make one as a "double" gift—holiday decoration and useful kitchen utensils after the season is past.

HOLLY KITCHEN WREATH

MATERIALS:
> **holly**
> **9"-diameter Styrofoam® or straw wreath form**
> **florist's pins**
> **ribbon**
> **small wooden kitchen utensils**
> **florist's picks**
> **wire**

Allow the freshly cut holly to soak for a few hours in water that is room temperature. Then cut holly into 2"- to 4"-long sprigs. Attach the sprigs to the wreath form with florist's pins, completely covering the wreath.

Cut ribbon into 8" lengths and tie around each utensil, making a bow. Wrap the wire from the florist's picks around each utensil; then push pick into the wreath form.

Attach a large bow to the top of the wreath. Wrap a short piece of wire around the top of the wreath and make a loop for hanging.

The pale gold of dried artichokes and dried flowers transforms an ordinary boxwood wreath into a stunning door decoration.

Even with the greenery and dried flower accent at the top, it is the shiny red cranberries that make this striking holiday wreath a surprise to all who approach the door.

CRANBERRY WREATH

MATERIALS:
  straw wreath form
  toothpicks
  fresh cranberries
  bow
  holly or other greenery
  statice or other dried flowers

Attach cranberries to the lower portion of the wreath form by breaking toothpicks into halves, inserting a toothpick half into the straw wreath form, then topping it with a firm cranberry. (Discard all overripe cranberries.) Insert the next toothpick half beside the first and continue until the lower half of the wreath is a mass of closely positioned cranberries. It is not necessary to put cranberries all around the wreath form since the back of the wreath will rest against a solid door or wall. Just attach the cranberries three-quarters of the way around the form.

Attach the bow to the top of the wreath with a florist's pick. Then, using the florist's picks again, attach greenery and dried flowers to the remaining portions of the wreath, balancing the arrangement on each side.

VINE WREATH

MATERIALS:
  honeysuckle, grapevine, or kudzu vines
  florist's wire
  apples, pomegranates, or other fruits and berries
  yarrow or other dried flowers
  large plaid bow

Start with a long, thick vine. Hold the thicker end of the vine in one hand and loop the vine as you would a garden hose into a circle about the size you want the finished wreath to be. On the next loop, pull the full length of the vine through the inside of the circle. Wrap the vine to the outside of the circle and pull it back through the inside in long spirals as shown in the diagram.

Some vines are fairly stiff, so you will be able to pull through the circle only about two times in each loop. However, the smaller, more flexible vines can be pulled through with the wraps much closer together; this will result in an obvious spiral pattern in the finished wreath. With the vines wrapped in and out in this way, the wreath will hold its shape without rope ties. Tuck ends of each vine securely inside the wreath.

Attach a piece of florist's wire to each piece of fruit by following the directions in Fruits & Berries, page 11. Push the ends of the wire through

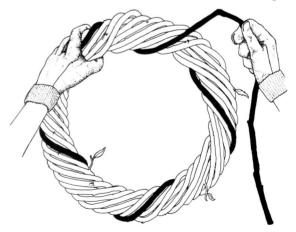

A spectacular vine wreath is as easy to make as a greenery wreath, and it will last for many years. Leave it unadorned or festooned with bright fruits and flowers. The graceful garland is constructed so that the greenery fans out from the "rope"—an appealing alternative to garlands in which the greenery lies in snug clusters around the door.

the wreath to the back and twist to secure each piece of fruit to the wreath.

Tuck small clusters of berries and yarrow or other dried flowers directly into the wreath, working the accents between vines to secure.

Wire a bright bow and a cluster of greenery to the bottom of the wreath. Make a loop of wire around the top of the wreath for hanging.

NUT & PINE CONE WREATH

MATERIALS:

5 lbs. assorted nuts (pecans, walnuts, almonds, filberts, etc.—use quite a lot of the filberts since they are used to fill "holes")
old nylon hose
20-30 medium-sized pine cones
1 roll medium-gauge florist's wire
24" diameter straw florist's wreath
florist's picks
2 cans spray polyurethane, gloss or satin finish
bow
heavy wire

The soft browns and golds of pine cones and nuts combine to make a holiday wreath that will last for years whether it is displayed indoors or out. A different, brightly colored bow can change the look from year to year.

Wrap nylon hose around one nut. Pull the nylon taut and twist; then tie the wire from the florist's pick around the twist; trim the hose approximately ¼" from the wire. (Do not cut small pieces of hose and wrap them around the nut; use the entire piece of hose and cut as you go.) Repeat the procedure for each nut to be used in the wreath. For a large wreath you will need approximately half a grocery bag full of wrapped nuts.

To make the pine cone "flowers," use a saw to cut the upper two-thirds off several of the pine cones; the remaining bottom portion resembles a "flower" and is attached to the wreath along with the other plain pine cones.

Wrap florist's wire around the wreath one time and twist tightly to secure. Without cutting the wire, continue to wrap it around the wreath, attaching the pine cones as you go by pulling the wire taut between the "petals" of the cones. The cones should be placed very closely together, nearly touching. Put more cones on the wreath than you think you need; they should cover approximately three-fourths of the surface of the wreath.

Using needlenose pliers to hold the florist's picks, insert the nuts in the empty spaces between the pine cones. Begin with the larger nuts

and use the smaller filberts to fill in the small spaces. To keep the wreath nicely rounded, do not push the nuts' picks all the way down to the wreath; instead, keep the nuts at the same level as the top of the cones.

Spray the wreath thoroughly with polyurethane, using several coats and allowing it to dry between coats. The polyurethane brings out the colors of the nuts and cones and preserves the wreath for future use.

To hang your wreath, wrap heavy wire around the wreath at the top and form a loop.

Attach a bow with a large florist's pick. After the holiday season is over, store the wreath inside a heavy duty plastic garbage bag and seal tightly with a fastener. (A piece of cardboard might be placed under the wreath for extra support.) To preserve the beauty of your bow, stuff tissue paper inside each individual loop.

Special Touches for the House

Easy Accents

Decorating your home for the Christmas season does not have to be expensive or time consuming. Nor should the decorations stand out in stark relief from the decor or comfortable feeling your home holds all year long. Instead of purchasing an elaborate decoration, sit down and add a little thoughtful creativity to the surroundings you already know and treasure.

A mantel ablaze with candles is not impossible because you don't have a large collection of candlesticks. Arrange red candles of different heights and thicknesses on jar lids and then amass greenery and ribbons around the bases. The effect is the same, and the cost is minimal.

Clusters of greenery from your yard and bright snatches of ribbon used effectively throughout your house can carry out the Christmas feeling in surprising ways.

The ideas shown in this section are truly "easy accents." The photographs show you simple and inexpensive ways to make the most out of what you have available in the yard, the attic, or right in your living room. Decorate your entire house using imagination and only a little bit of time.

Traditional and graceful hurricane shades take on new sparkle for the holidays. Cluster varied sizes down the center of your table and then fill them to the brim with ornaments, tiny packages or toys, or even pine cones or fruit.

Above: Ribbons and bows can bring the holiday mood to the most unexpected places. Here cheerful red bows encircle each light on this handsome chandelier.

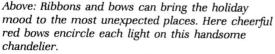

Top right: The simplest ideas are often the most spectacular. Soft fabric bows encircle the everyday throw pillows on this couch, transforming each into a holiday surprise package.

Right: Red candles, red apples, red berries, and a bright bow to "wrap" the mirror—the inventive assembling of these festive items makes the seasonal best of the things you already have. In an entry hall, a living or dining room—wherever you have a mirror over furniture—this abundance of holiday reds and the warmth of gold will brighten the Christmas scene.

20

Above: Poinsettias are one of the brightest and most cheerful signs of the Christmas season. Their colorful bracts in shades of pinks, creams, and reds usually last a long time if kept near a sunny window. After the plant has shed its leaves, cut back each stem so that it is left with only two leaf scars. Move the plants to a cool, dark place and do not water. When all danger of frost is past, plunge the pot up to the rim into the soil outdoors, water thoroughly, and feed. Cut back long stems to encourage bushy growth.

To force the poinsettia into bloom for the 1982 holiday season, place the plant in a dark closet for 14 hours a day beginning 6 weeks prior to the date you wish it to flower.

༄ༀ

Left: This Norfolk Island pine is at home beside the stairway throughout the year, but for the holidays it wears a colorful dress of tiny lights, lightweight ornaments, and puffy bows.

Above: Use a single tree to brighten an end table, or arrange a forest of them down the center of your dining table. Wedge a cone of florist's foam into a dish to hold water. Then, starting at the top, poke boxwood sprigs into the foam until the tree is thick and evenly shaped. Decorate the miniature tree with perky bows and bits of baby's breath.

လပ်က

Top: Diagonal garlands set a festive mood on the dining table in the eighteenth-century Hammond-Harwood House in Annapolis, Maryland. The base may be made of Styrofoam® (with felt underneath) and covered with greenery, fruits, and berries.

Above: Osage Oranges, fragrant cedar sprigs, and shiny magnolia leaves—all familiar materials of the South—form a pyramid of holiday greens that is striking for its different textures. To duplicate this conversation piece from Dallas's Old City Park, poke florist's picks into each osage orange and insert into a Styrofoam® pyramid base.

လပ်က

Top: Only Santa Claus (or a grandparent) would leave such a deliciously tempting centerpiece on your table. Styrofoam® wedged into a large silver bowl holds lollipop sticks firmly in place.

Charming nut baskets were popular during the Victorian era to hold cards or sewing. This is an inventive way to recycle old baskets, and filled with fresh greenery, nuts, fruit, or a favorite jar of preserves, the baskets become treasured gifts.

NUT BASKET

MATERIALS:
acorns, peach or prune pits, seedpods, etc.
old basket
brown linoleum paste
hemlock cones
petals of large sugar pine cones
felt
white glue

Bake acorns or any other nuts picked up off the ground in a 200° oven for 1 hour to kill any worms.

Start at the bottom of the basket and slather on a generous amount of linoleum paste. Working in rows from the bottom up, push hemlock cones, acorns, peach and prune pits, and seed pods into the paste, placing some things on end for interest. Stop halfway down the basket and allow to dry; the weight of the nuts and cones can push out the lower rows if you work too rapidly.

If your basket has any broken places, patch with cardboard; the basket will be covered on the outside with nuts and on the inside with the felt lining.

Complete the upper half and handle of the basket in the same manner as the bottom. Cover the top rim of the basket with overlapping petals of the large sugar pine cone.

Cut a felt lining to fit the inside of the basket and glue in place.

Note: For a 24-page booklet of designer Sunny O'Neil's *Favorite Christmas Decorations*, send $1.75 (postpaid) to Sunny O'Neil, 7106 River Road, Bethesda, MD 20034.

Mantels & Windows

Christmastime brings warm visions of family and friends gathered around the fireplace, the natural focal point for holiday get-togethers. The effects you create on the mantel itself or on the wall over the mantel can be a subtle extension of the holiday mood you've balanced throughout the room, or the mantel can be a decorative show-stopper, rivaled only by the Christmas tree.

The hearth should say "welcome" to all those we invite to share our holidays. And although a mantel laden with greenery and candles is a simple yet striking arrangement, the photographs shown here offer a few alternate ideas for individualizing your mantel decorations.

Windows, too, can play a special role in holiday decorating because they allow those inside and outside to appreciate virtually the same arrangement. A cluster of foliage, a cheerful ribbon, a candle—all of these reflect the good cheer within a room and extend the spirit of the season to those who pass by.

ઉ૬૦

Top right: Oyster shells and pomegranates comprise a unique holiday mantel decoration that is in keeping with the coastal area. The shells, fruit, and greenery are wired to Styrofoam® and attached to the mantel molding in Hammond-Harwood House.

ઉ૬૦

Right: Fresh flowers and garden greenery—here in a formally balanced composition—create an elegant effect on this marble mantel. Christmas poinsettias in white and pink echo the colors of the room and add a seasonal touch to the arrangements.

ઉ૬૦

Left: A grapevine wreath—against a Christmas red wall that seems made to order for the season—hangs above a mantel filled to overflowing with a tumble of large pine cones. For instructions on making a vine wreath, see page 16. Sprigs of baby's breath and narrow gold ribbon soften the very individual arrangement.

A shining brass candlestick with a red candle and bow is surrounded by delicate greenery in this simple seasonal statement on a windowsill. Greenbrier smilax will keep about two weeks out of water, and ivy would also be effective.

Evergreen sprigs and an elegant bow of gold satin brighten a double-hung window. Wire around the lock holds this simple window arrangement in place.

Children will delight in helping to make this Christmas a white one by transforming delicate roadside blossoms of Queen Anne's Lace into "snowflakes" for the window or tree. These dazzling patterns are so complex they could only have come from nature.

QUEEN ANNE'S LACE ORNAMENTS

MATERIALS:
 Queen Anne's Lace blossoms
 spray adhesive
 white diamond dust glitter
 narrow satin ribbon, white or off-white
 white glue

Remove stems from the Queen Anne's Lace. Place about four blossoms on a page in your telephone book; allow ½" of pages between layers to serve as a cushion. Weight the telephone book and put in a warm, dry place for about 1 week.

Spray both sides of each pressed blossom with spray adhesive; then cover both sides with glitter. (White paint may be substituted for the spray adhesive if the blossoms have a yellowish tint.)

Tie a ribbon loop with a bow on top and glue the bottom of the loop to the back of each blossom.

Note: For a 24-page booklet of designer Sunny O'Neil's *Favorite Christmas Decorations*, send $1.75 (postpaid) to Sunny O'Neil, 7106 River Road, Bethesda, MD 20034.

Christmas Trees

Selecting the Right Tree

The unexpected color of Colorado blue spruce creates a dramatic Christmas tree, but sharp needles make it somewhat difficult to decorate. Sprigs of baby's breath give this tree a soft, snowflakelike effect.

When children look at a Christmas tree, they see perfection; they never notice the branches that are a bit uneven or the lights that are not perfectly arranged. To them, a Christmas tree is magical and filled with expectations of approaching delights. Even for those of us who have to think about such practical details as needles shedding on the floor, a Christmas tree is still enchanting. But there are a few guidelines to follow when purchasing your tree that will help eliminate some of the problems and make your selection a wise one.

The length of time you keep your tree, the way you decorate it, and the dimensions of your room will all affect the kind of Christmas tree you need. Christmas trees are also getting more expensive every year, so to get your money's worth, you should buy the type of tree best suited to your needs.

The first consideration in selecting any cut Christmas tree is freshness. If the tree is dropping needles when you buy it, it is almost sure to lose them all before the season is over. When you purchase a Christmas tree, feel the foliage to make sure it is pliable, and shake the tree to check for dropping needles. Brittle or shedding foliage is an indication of excessive dryness, a condition that greatly increases the potential fire hazard.

The length of time you plan to keep your Christmas tree should influence the type you choose. The firs are generally the longest lasting, especially the Fraser and noble firs. These trees maintain their foliage for 6 to 8 weeks after cutting, so they are perfect for the family that keeps a tree throughout the entire holiday season. Balsam fir, perhaps the most common Christmas tree, is usually less expensive than the Fraser and noble firs and should maintain its foliage for at least a month inside the house.

Scotch pine is another good choice for the long-term Christmas tree. It may, in fact, be longer lasting than the firs. Unfortunately, the foliage of Scotch pine tends to lose its dark green color after several weeks indoors. Fading to a dull gray green, the needles tend to become dry and brittle, but they do remain attached for quite some time.

The spruces are popular Christmas trees, but they are not dependable for more than a few weeks.

Red cedar is the traditional Christmas tree in the South, but along with other old-fashioned favorites such as hemlock, Virginia pine, and white pine, red cedar dries out very quickly and should be selected only if you plan to keep the tree for less than a week.

Color is another consideration. Not all Christmas trees are green. Some are dark green, some are light green, and a few are even silvery or blue. The grayish-green color of the Douglas fir or the distinctive foliage of the Colorado blue spruce presents an entirely different effect from a dark green Virginia pine or the yellow green Norway spruce and red cedar.

The way you decorate your tree will also have a bearing on the kind of tree you choose. A dense tree such as a Scotch pine is a good choice if you do not have a lot of ornaments, but if your collection is sizable, select a more open tree such as a fir or spruce.

Do not forget the overall size of the tree. Christmas trees look smaller on an open lot, so measure the height of your ceiling and the width of the area where you plan to put it before you go tree shopping.

No matter which type of Christmas tree you choose, it is essential to condition the tree before you decorate. Once a tree is cut, the microscopic channels in the trunk become clogged with sap and air. In order for the tree to absorb water, you must cut off at least 2″ of the trunk. The tree should then be placed in a container of water, deep enough to cover at least 4″ of the base. If possible, allow the tree to soak overnight before bringing it indoors.

A source of water throughout the holidays is essential to prolonging freshness. A number of reservoir-type stands are available; for best results, select one with at least a 2-quart capacity.

Above: For smaller rooms, the upright-growing red spruce fits easily into a corner.

❧

Top insert: Noble fir is easy for children to decorate because of its soft, pliable needles and broad, shelf-like branches. This fir is also a good choice if you have large decorations, such as these handmade ornaments and snowflakes.

❧

Right insert: The upright, spreading form and fragrant foliage of balsam fir have made it one of the most popular trees for Christmas. Its open branches make it easy to decorate.

❧

Opposite: Scotch pine holds its needles longer than almost any other cut tree. Although it tends to dry out rather quickly, the foliage will remain attached for several months.

Shell Collector's Tree

So much of the South is within easy reach of the ocean that shell collecting has become a favorite pastime. But seashells don't have to mean summer and sand; each of nature's designs is so striking in shape and color that the shells should be used all year long as decorative accents for the home. If your collection includes the small, fairly lightweight shells that are common to most beaches, why not create a spectacular display by decorating this year's Christmas tree with the delicate colors of the ocean's jewels?

Although the seashells alone are perfect Christmas ornaments, you may wish to create a more romantic touch by adding ribbons and tiny pearls to the shells as shown on this shell collector's balsam tree.

Note: To order a set of four shell and pearl ornaments, with white satin ribbon (shown in the photograph), send a check or money order for $12.00 (plus $1.50 postage and handling) to American Sampler, 2106 Flowerwood Drive, Birmingham, Alabama 35244. (Alabama residents add .48 tax.)

SHELL AND PEARL ORNAMENTS

MATERIALS:
   seashells. Choose shells that are light in weight and are basically flat and fan shaped.
   simulated pearls. Five pearls in 3 different sizes are used for each shell for a graduated effect.
   527 Multi-purpose Cement®. This is available in most craft stores.
   findings. This is the term applied to the metal attachments inserted through the hole in the shell. Use either a locket bail hanger or a split jump ring, available at craft stores.
   narrow satin ribbon
   ornament hangers. Use standard Christmas ornament hooks or gold thread.
   electric drill and 1/16″ bit

Place shell face (round side) down on a scrap piece of board. (You will drill on the inside of the shell cup.) Grasp the shell firmly with one hand and position the drill bit on the shell ⅛″ to ¼″ from the top of the shell. Drill through the shell and into the board, holding the drill at a right angle to the shell.

To attach the locket bail finding, press so that both points go through the hole in the shell. To attach the split jump ring, open the ring with pliers, insert through the hole in the shell, and close with pliers.

Put 5 small drops of cement along the bottom front edge of the shell and allow to set 1 to 2 minutes. Press the pearls in place, the largest in the center and smallest at the outsides. Allow to dry for 2 to 3 hours.

Loop ribbon through the finding and tie a bow. Attach ornament hanger or metallic thread.

Left: Four perfect choices for decorating your tree with seashells: Pectin swifti (the largest shell with delicate pink and white colors), Mexican flat (brownish pink), Japanese cups (white), and Pectin pallium (the smallest shell with plum-wine colors).

꒒꒖꒒

Right: Add sparkle and variety to your shell tree with gold-painted starfish. Simply glue a finding to one point and add a bow of narrow gold cord.

A crisp white sand dollar of any size is a natural ornament for a Christmas tree—and one with a ready-made hole. A bright red ribbon adds a Christmasy touch.

To complement the delicate shades and romantic feeling of your seashell tree, tuck dried hydrangeas among the shell-laden branches. Accent the bouquets with satin ribbons.

Birds' Nests Tree

What is more natural than birds' nests perched on tree branches, even if it is a Christmas tree? This particularly individualized decoration is in the home of a nest collector who, since childhood, has marveled at the distinguishing sizes, shapes, and surprising compositions of these tiny homes. Her collection—complete with tiny *faux* eggs—is tucked in among an assortment of other such natural decorations as walnut ornaments, bleached pine cones, berry clusters, and spice ornaments, all on a blue spruce. The result is a striking Christmas celebration of nature.

Instructions follow for creating both the walnut and spice ornaments and for bleaching the pine cones. The splashes of bright red are easily achieved by draping clusters of cotoneaster berries over the branches. Tiny white lights, a few golden stars, and a garland of narrow gold ribbon add just the right amount of sparkle.

SPICE ORNAMENTS

MATERIALS:
  ¼"-thick Styrofoam® sheets or corrugated
    cardboard
  brown florist's tape
  white glue
  ¼"-wide gold braid
  toothpicks
  spices (poppyseeds, whole cloves, whole
    allspice, etc.)
  small dried flowers
  thin gold cord

Cut out a circle or heart shape with scissors from either Styrofoam® or cardboard, using a cookie cutter as a pattern if desired. Completely cover the cut-out with floral tape. Run a fine line of glue around the very edge and circle with gold braid. Loop the gold cord at the top to act as a hanger, securing the ends with glue and a short straight pin.

Spices may be arranged in various designs and in combination with dried flowers. (To make a solid gray brown background, brush glue over the entire surface and then press the ornament face down into poppy seeds.) Dab spots of glue on the ornament with a toothpick; then use tweezers to position the spices and flowers. Let dry thoroughly.

BLEACHED PINE CONES

MATERIALS:
  dry, open pine cones
  household bleach
  thin gold thread

Place pine cones in the bottom of a plastic container and pour in enough bleach to cover the cones completely. You may need to put a scrap piece of wood on top of the cones to keep them from floating and becoming mottled.

Allow the cones to soak overnight in the bleach. In the morning, drain the bleach and put the cones in a warm, dry place; they will open out as they dry.

Attach the cones to the tree by wrapping thin gold thread around the petals at the base and then tying a loop.

WALNUT ORNAMENTS

MATERIALS:
  walnut shells
  white glue
  thin gold cord
  small dried flowers
  spices (whole cloves, allspice, etc.)
  narrow ribbon

Crack walnuts very carefully into perfect halves and remove nutmeats. Glue the halves back together, inserting a loop of gold cord or a narrow ribbon at the top to act as a hanger. When dry, dab more glue around the top. Arrange flowers and spices to form a little cluster. Make a tiny bow with ribbon and attach with more glue. Let dry. (An empty egg carton makes a good storage box for these ornaments.)

Above: Red, ripe clusters of coton-easter berries seem a natural accent around birds' nests and pine cones in a Christmas tree designed by Nature.

❦

Bottom left: For a Christmas tree with a fragrance as intriguing as its appearance, make these easy spice ornaments. Lacy accents of dried flowers and pine cone "petals" make the ornaments as appealing as their aroma.

❦

Bottom right: Christmas and walnuts are an expected combination. But by recycling the shells into charming ornaments, you can enjoy the nuts long after the nutmeats are eaten.

Fruit & Berry Tree

Tangerines, lemons, limes, and nandina berries festoon this 4'-tall table-top blue spruce. The tree is alive, complete with root ball and dirt, and is temporarily potted for the holidays in a large terra cotta pot filled with pine bark. Southern magnolia branches with sharpened stems are poked into the pine bark which conceals the root ball.

The branches of the blue spruce are very stiff, an important characteristic because they must support the weight of the fruit.

Freshness is the key both to purchasing and to decorating a Christmas tree such as this, particularly if you want the display to last throughout the holidays. Be sure to water your tree frequently during the season. Select firm fruit with no bruises or cuts. The berries should also be firm and bright red.

Follow the simple directions below to hang the fresh fruit and to make the nandina and sweet gum ball ornaments. The remaining flourishes on the tree in the photograph are sprays of dried baby's breath and small, pecan-filled bags of tulle tied to the branches with bright red bows. The tree is crowned with a pomegranate.

FRUIT ORNAMENTS

MATERIALS:
  fresh tangerines, lemons, and limes
  dark green chenille stems

Cut a small "X" with a sharp knife at the stem end of each piece of fruit. Insert a chenille stem through the hole, pushing it into the fruit as far as possible.

Make a hook at the top of the chenille stem to hang the fruit from the branches.

Fresh fruit in cheerful oranges, yellows, and greens is intermingled with interesting "spiky" ornaments made from sweet gum balls and red nandina berries. Both ideas are inexpensive and unbreakable.

NANDINA & SWEET GUM BALLS

MATERIALS:
  dry sweet gum balls
  spray floral adhesive
  firm nandina berries
  green sewing thread

Spray each sweet gum ball with floral adhesive, thoroughly coating all sides of the ball. Poke nandina berries between the points of each sweet gum ball and allow the adhesive to dry. Wrap thread around each sweet gum ball twice; then make a loop for hanging.

Christmas Bazaar

azaars abound at Christmastime. It is also a time when we are most creative. Whether you turn your energies to making ornaments or gifts for sale at a community or Church bazaar or craft show, or whether you are looking for ideas to enrich your own holidays, this chapter is filled with surprising suggestions for decorations, ornaments, and gifts.

The make-it-yourself ideas in "Easy Holiday Crafts" are just that—easy. A variety of needlework techniques is represented in this section—cross-stitch, crochet, appliqué, etc.—but there are also fun crafts that require little more than glue, pins, and an hour of time.

Holiday projects to busy little fingers are featured in a special "Children's Workshop"—three great craft ideas to help them join in the excitement of the season by making decorations for their family or class tree or by making those very "personalized" gifts mother and dad treasure for years. Many ideas throughout this chapter would make wonderful group projects—ideal for classmates or scout troops to make together before their Christmas break.

"Wraps & Cards" is a section intended to help you solve a few of the unusual wrapping problems we all encounter those last, busy weeks before Christmas. Suggestions and instructions are given for tissue paper sacks for large or irregularly shaped gifts, specially tailored bags for wine and other spirits, and fabric boxes filled with temptations from the kitchen. There even is an inventive way to decorate boxes that will be mailed. A few how-to ideas are also included for individualizing this year's Christmas cards and gift tags. Mailing tips and a packaging chart from the U.S. postal service will help your packages to arrive undamaged and on time.

From an elegant Christmas red and lace table runner to cuddly animal dolls for peeking out of a stocking, "Christmas Bazaar" is designed to help you personalize your decorations and your gift giving.

Easy Holiday Crafts

Festive Linens

Nothing is merrier than a beautifully appointed table or buffet laden with tempting goodies. Lengthwise strips of lace dress up this otherwise plain runner, and handsome lace-edged napkins were appliquéd with narrow strips of the runner fabric, creating a matched set of table linens.

MATERIALS:
> **fabric for runner and trim on napkins**
> **wide lace the length of the runner**
> **narrow lace twice the length of the runner**
> **wide lace to trim napkins**
> **set of napkins**

To determine the size of your runner, first measure the length of your buffet or table. Decide on the amount of overhang you want for each end (12″ is the usual). Add twice the overhang measurement to the length of the buffet; then add 1″ for hem allowances. (Example: a buffet 42″ long would require a length of fabric 42″ plus 24″ plus 1″ for a total length of 67″.)

To decide the width of the runner, measure the depth of the buffet (15″ to 18″ is usual for a buffet; slightly wider for a table). Add 1″ for hems to the width measurement.

Before cutting, preshrink both the fabric (if it is washable) and the lace. Press and cut the fabric to the determined size. Press and cut both the wide and narrow lace to the length of the fabric.

Center and pin the wide lace along the length of fabric, measuring carefully to be sure it is exactly in the middle. Baste the wide lace to the runner. Pin and baste a row of narrow lace parallel to each edge of the center strip; keep measuring carefully. Sew the three lengths of lace to the fabric with a straight or zigzag stitch.

To finish the runner, fold under all four raw edges ¼″ and press. Fold under ¼″ again, press, and stitch.

Matching napkins are easy to create and would complete the holiday setting. To add lace borders to a set of plain napkins, position a length of wide lace along one edge of a napkin, right sides together. (Be sure to allow enough excess of lace at the starting point to be able to miter that last corner.) Using a zigzag stitch, sew the lace to the napkin along the edge. Fold the lace to a mitered corner and continue sewing to the next corner. Repeat around the napkin, mitering each corner. Press the lace and napkin, and then add trim over the seam edges.

To trim the napkins, cut 1″-wide bias strips from the same fabric as the runner. Turn under ¼″ on each side of the strip and press. Sew the fabric strips with a zigzag stitch just inside the lace border, mitering the corners. You may prefer to trim the napkins with matching ribbon instead of bias strips.

Jewels for the Tree

Garage-sale "jewels," dime-store "finds," and a little imagination can bring glitter and elegance to your Christmas tree. This is a great project to share with children—and the results are really quite stunning.

MATERIALS:
   Styrofoam® balls
   velvet or satin ribbon
   long straight pins
   narrow metallic trim (rickrack or braid)
   pearl beads, glass beads, sequins—any "jewels"
   white glue
   pearl-headed pins

Divide each ball into 4 equal sections with velvet or satin ribbon. Pin the ribbon in place and add narrow metallic trim over the top of the ribbon. Fill in the 4 sections with small beads or sequins, using straight pins that are dipped first in glue.

For the top and bottom of each ball, string sequins and beads over pearl-headed pins. Insert at the top and bottom in a circle to cover the raw edges of the ribbon.

To hang the ball, make a 6″ loop of ribbon. Insert a pearl-headed pin through the ends, dip the pin in glue, and insert at the top of the ball.

Use a pearl-headed pin (or a hat pin) for the bottom of the ball, adding slightly larger beads and sequins.

Gold Crocheted Ornaments

Rich golden hearts and wreaths bring a romantic Victorian touch to your decorations. Crochet your favorites to trim your tree and to wear as pendants for holiday partying.

MATERIALS:
   heavy gold metallic yarn (1 spool makes about 5 or 6 ornaments)
   size 4 steel crochet hook

TERMS: ch (chain), st (stitch), sl st (slip stitch), sc (single crochet), dc (double crochet), hdc (half double crochet), tr (triple crochet), htr (half triple crochet), dtr (double triple crochet), yo (yarn over).

Note: People who crochet may not be familiar with the htr (half triple crochet) stitch. See diagram for this stitch.

HEART
Ch 6, sl st into first ch to form ring.
   Round 1: Ch 5, * dc into ring, ch 2. Repeat from * 8 times. Sl st into 3rd ch of 5 ch.
   Round 2: Ch 3, 2 dc in ch 2 space. * 3 dc in next ch 2 space. Repeat from * 8 times. Sl st into 3rd ch (30 dc).
   Round 3: * sc in first dc of preceding round, hdc in next st, ch 1, dc, ch 1, htr, ch 1, tr, ch 1,

dtr, ch 1, tr, ch 1, htr, ch 1, dc, ch 1, hdc, ch 1, sc, ch 1, hdc, ch 1, dc, ch 1, htr, ch 1 * tr, ch 1. Reverse stitch order between * for 2nd half of heart. Sl st in top of heart (last stitch of preceding round).

Round 4: Sl st in top of sc. * 3 sc in first ch 1 space. Repeat from * 11 times. 4 sc in each of next 2 ch 1 space. 3 sc in next 12 ch 1 space. Sl st into top of last sc of preceding round. Sl st into top of heart.

Round 5: * ch 4. Skip 3 st and dc into next st. (3rd sc of preceding round.) Repeat from * 4 times. * 2 ch 4, skip 3 st, sc. Repeat from * 2 three times. * 3 ch 4, skip 2 st, dc. Repeat from * 3 once. Ch 4, skip 2 st, sc. * 4 ch 4, skip 3 st, sc. *4 repeat twice. *5 ch 4, skip 3 st, dc. Repeat from * 5 four times. Ch 4, sl st into last sc of preceding round.

Round 6: Ch 6. Turn. Sc into 2nd ch 4 space in preceding round. * ch 6, sc into next ch 4 space. Repeat from *7 times. Ch 9, skip bottom loop of heart, sc into next space. * ch 6, sc into next space. Repeat from * 7 times. Ch 6, sl st into first st of preceding round. Ch 1. Turn.

Round 7: * 2 sc, 2 hdc, 1 dc, 2 hdc, 2 sc, into ch 6 loop. Repeat from * 7 times. 3 sc, 1 hdc into next loop. 1 sc, 1 hdc, 1 dc, 1 htr, 1 dc, 1 hdc, 1 sc into bottom loop of heart. 1 hdc, 3 sc into next loop. Repeat stitches between * for next 8 loops.

WREATH

Ch 45, sl st into first ch to form ring.

Round 1: 80 sc into ring. Join last sc to first with sl st.

Round 2: Ch 5 * skip 1 st, dc into next st, ch 2. Repeat from * 38 times. Sl st into 3rd ch of 5 ch (counts as 1 dc—40 dc total).

Round 3: * ch 9, sc into 3rd ch 2 space of preceding round. 1 hdc, 1 dc into same space. 1 tr into top of dc, 1 dc, 1 hdc, 1 sc into next ch 2 space. Repeat from * 9 times.

Round 4: * 7 sc in 9 ch loop of preceding round. Ch 2, sl st in top of tr, ch 2. Repeat from * 9 times. Sl st into first sc of round.

Round 5: * ch 12, sl st into first ch 2 space of preceding round. Ch 5, sl st into next ch 2 space. Repeat 9 times.

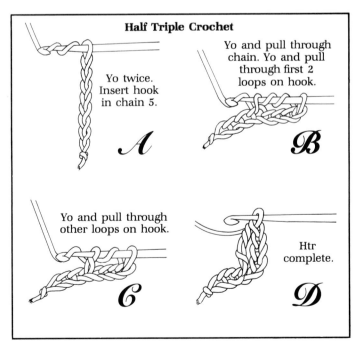

Half Triple Crochet

A — Yo twice. Insert hook in chain 5.

B — Yo and pull through chain. Yo and pull through first 2 loops on hook.

C — Yo and pull through other loops on hook.

D — Htr complete.

Pearl-Beaded Snowflakes

Even if your Christmas can't be white outside, what could be more magical than delicate, pearl snowflakes glistening on your Christmas tree? These ornaments would also be stunning as package decorations—or hanging in front of a frosty windowpane.

Note: Work on a padded surface such as a shallow box lid covered with about four thicknesses of cloth.

MATERIALS:
  12 (5mm × 7mm) oat beads (O)
  168 (4mm) round beads (A)
  12 (2½mm) round beads (C)
  transparent nylon thread
  beading needle
  24- or 26-gauge wire

Round 1: String 12 A beads with nylon thread into a ring. Go through the ring a second time to tighten. Tie a double knot using the raw end and

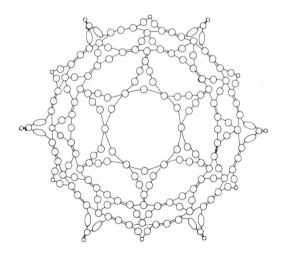

the remainder of the thread. (Take care not to pull the chain too taut.) Work raw end into the ring. When the thread becomes short, tie a new length to the end you have been using and work the knot into the beads.

Round 2: String AAAA to begin forming the inside set of points; return through the next-to-last bead strung, and string AA; skip over one A on the inside ring and into the next A. (See diagram.) Do this 6 times around the circle. Go through the first 4 beads of the first point made in Round 2.

Round 3: String AAAAA between the top beads of every point made in Round 2. Go through the top bead of the last point and the first 2 beads of the first chain made in Round 3.

Round 4: String AAA; skip middle bead of AAAAA chain made in Round 3; go through 2 beads. Make another AAA peak over the first peak made in Round 2. Do this 6 times for a total of 12 peaks; then go through the first 2 beads of the first peak made in Round 4.

Round 5: String AAA between the top beads of

every peak made in Round 4; then go through the first AAA chain made in Round 5.

Round 6: String ACA; skip the top bead of the peaks made in Round 4; go through the AAA chain made in Round 5. Then string OAC into a point; return through A; string O; skip the top bead of the peak made in Round 4. Do this 6 times, alternating short peaks and long points.

When the snowflake is completed, string wire through the last chain (outside row) to make firm. It is best to work from one point of the snowflake to the next, being careful not to allow any kinks in the wire. The wire should overlap at least ¼" inside the beads at the finishing point.

Work thread into one of the points to attach a loop for hanging.

Cross-Stitched Lids

Your home-canned specialty becomes two gifts when you add a cross-stitched lid. If you're not yet famous for a special jam, jelly, or preserve, try one of the recipes in "Celebrations from the Kitchen." A particularly delicious favorite is the Peach-Pecan Jam (recipe on page 92).

MATERIALS:
5" square of No. 14 Aida cloth
5" square of sheer-weight fusible interfacing
1 skein each of DMC embroidery floss 3371 brown-black and 666 red
wide-mouth canning jar with cap and band
white household glue
embroidery needle
clear plastic lens (optional)

Follow the chart to cross-stitch the design on Aida cloth with 2 ply of the 6-ply floss.

Follow the package directions on the fusible interfacing to iron onto the back of the worked piece.

Trim the cloth to fit the jar lid, centering the design. Glue cloth in place. Unscrew band from sealed food and slip covered lid on top of sealed lid; replace screw-on band.

If desired, a clear plastic lens may be used to protect the cross-stitched design; simply place it over the cloth and then screw on the band.

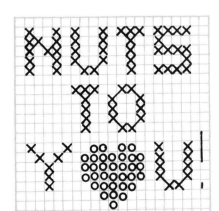

DMC Color Code
X 3371 brown-black
O 666 red

41

Calico Christmas Tree

Make a Christmas centerpiece that will last for years. Decorate your calico tree with yellow stars or miniature wooden ornaments, or wrap tiny packages to tuck in among the branches.

MATERIALS:

3¼ yards (45"-wide) calico or other printed fabric
polyester fiberfill
scraps of fabric for star and hearts

To enlarge the pattern for the tree, prepare a grid of 1" squares. Number the squares vertically and horizontally on both the pattern and your grid. Use the numbers as a guide to copy the pattern from the original to your grid, square by square.

Fold the fabric in half lengthwise and follow the cutting guide to cut 3 shapes on the fold line and 3 shapes with ⅜" seam allowances along the selvedge. With right sides facing, sew the half-tree shapes together to form 3 seamed shapes.

Sew 2 tree shapes, right sides together, using a short stitch ⅜" from the edge. At the base, leave an opening as indicated by the notches. Repeat for the other 4 tree shapes.

Trim the seam and clip at the points of the branches. Turn all 3 sections of tree right side out. Carefully push out points from the inside, using a large needle. Steam press.

Topstitch ¼" from the outside edge on all 3 sections of the tree, using a longer stitch. You now have 3 finished tree shapes. Lay one on top of the other; stitch down the center from the top of the tree to the base, using a short stitch. Reinforce the stitching several times.

Push fiberfill into all points; then stuff the tree. Whipstitch the openings closed at the base.

For each star or heart, cut 2 pieces. Sew with right sides together, stitching ¼" from the edge and leaving open as indicated on the pattern. Turn and stuff. Whipstitch openings closed and tack to the tree. Use larger hearts near the bottom and smaller ones near the top.

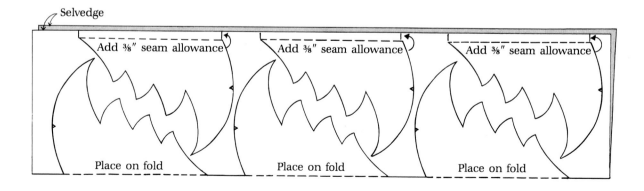

Selvedge

Add ⅜" seam allowance   Add ⅜" seam allowance   Add ⅜" seam allowance

Place on fold   Place on fold   Place on fold

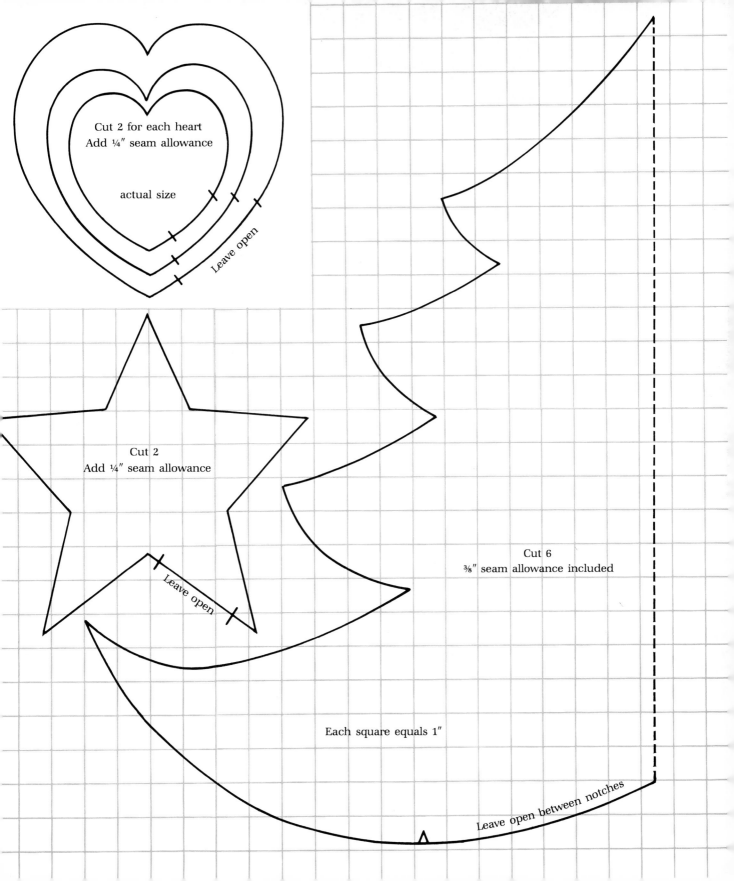

Cut 2 for each heart
Add ¼″ seam allowance

actual size

Leave open

Cut 2
Add ¼″ seam allowance

Leave open

Cut 6
⅜″ seam allowance included

Each square equals 1″

Leave open between notches

Appliquéd Stockings

Hung traditionally "by the chimney with care," these stockings are entirely machine stitched. The 20″ stockings are roomy enough to take a lot of stuffing—by Santa, of course.

MATERIALS:

Santa Stocking:
  1 yard 45″-wide green calico fabric
  1 yard polyester batting
  1 yard 45″-wide white fabric
  ½ yard pregathered white eyelet trim
  scrap of red calico fabric (for chimney)
  scrap of red fabric (for Santa's hat and suit)
  scrap of pink fabric (for Santa's face)
  red, white, and black thread
  6″ red grosgrain ribbon

Christmas Tree Stocking:
  1 yard 45″-wide red fabric
  1 yard polyester batting
  ½ yard 45″-wide white fabric
  ½ yard 45″-wide green calico fabric (for tree)
  ½ yard pregathered white eyelet trim
  scrap of brown fabric (for rocking horse)
  3 (2″ × 2″) scraps of 3 different calico fabrics (for gifts)
  red, green, white, and golden brown thread
  6″ red grosgrain ribbon

Using the diagram as a guide, cut a stocking and a cuff pattern from brown paper. (Be sure to reverse the stocking shape when cutting the fabric for the back of the stocking.)

For the Santa Stocking: Cut 2 stocking shapes from green calico, 2 from batting, and 2 from white fabric for lining. Using the cuff pattern, cut 1 from batting and 2 from white fabric.

For the Christmas Tree Stocking: Cut 2 stocking shapes from red fabric, 2 from batting, and 2 from white fabric for lining. Using the cuff pattern, cut 1 from batting and 2 from green calico.

Pin the outside fabric of both stocking shapes to the batting and then the lining; use these pieces as one when assembling the stocking.

Stitch the cuff across the top of each stocking piece, the wrong side of the cuff to the right side of the stocking. Cut the battings for cuffs in half. Hold one-half of the batting against the cuff; fold the top of the cuff over the batting to the front of the stocking. Turn under the raw edge ¼″ and press. Pin a 9″-long piece of eyelet trim just under the pressed edge and topstitch.

To enlarge patterns for the appliqué pieces, prepare a grid of 1″ squares. Number squares vertically and horizontally on both the pattern and your grid. Use the numbers as a guide to copy the pattern outline from the original onto your grid, square by square. Make a pattern for each appliqué shape out of brown paper.

Pin pattern pieces for appliqué on the following fabrics: *For the Santa Stocking:* Santa's beard, trim on hat and cuffs, and snow on and under chimney from white; chimney from red calico; Santa's hat and suit from red; and Santa's face from pink. *For the Christmas Tree Stocking:* tree

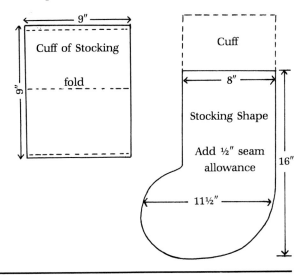

continued

from green calico; rocking horse from brown; and gifts from 3 different calico fabrics.

Cut out the appliqué pieces.

Using a narrow zigzag stitch, machine-appliqué pieces to the front of the *Santa Stocking* in the following order: Santa's suit, chimney, snow on and under the chimney, cuffs, beard, face, hat, and trim. *For the Christmas Tree Stocking,* machine-appliqué the tree, the horse, and then the gifts.

Machine embroider the details with a narrow zigzag stitch. *For the Santa Stocking:* eyes in black thread, mustache and ball on hat in white thread. *For Christmas Tree Stocking:* tree garlands and one gift ribbon in red thread; halter, horse's eye, and tree's star in golden brown

thread; and remaining two gift ribbons in green thread. Check pattern for placement of machine embroidery.

To make a loop for hanging, double the pieces of ribbon and pin the ends 1½" down from the top of the cuff and facing inward on the front of the stocking.

Assemble the stockings by placing right sides together. Stitch around the stockings, using ½" seams. Clip curves, turn stockings to the right side, and press.

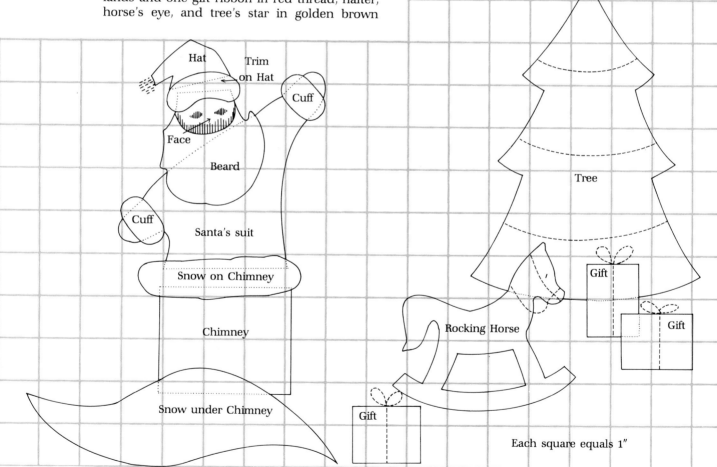

Each square equals 1"

46

Animal Dolls

Pocket-sized animal dolls are perfect stocking stuffers, adornments for packages under the tree, or as ornaments on the tree itself! Personalize the dolls for the pint-sized members of your family by creating different "accessories" for the dolls to hug.

MATERIALS:
  9″ × 12″ piece of velour or other fabric with a velvetlike nap (for each doll)
  scraps of felt (for ears and facial features)
  polyester fiberfill
  white glue
  embroidery thread, liquid embroidery pens, or felt-tip markers
  6″ × 12″ piece of fabric (for each doll dress)
  scraps of ribbon and lace (for trim on dress)
  scraps of fabric (for accessories)

Trace patterns and cut body, head, arms, ears (if making rabbit), and tail (if making raccoon) from velour fabric. Cut ears for other animals from felt. (Diagram A, page 48.)

Note: To make raccoon tail, cut a 3″ × 2¼″ rectangle from velour. Round one end of the rectangle. Make narrow zigzag stitches (on right side of fabric) about ¼″ apart across the width of the rectangle, using black or navy blue thread. Fold rectangle widthwise, right sides together, and stitch, leaving straight edge at top open. Turn to right side and stuff with fiberfill.

On the right side of the piece to be used for the face, lightly mark the position of facial features and ears with pencil or tailor's chalk. Pin the body and head (front) together at the neck, right sides facing. Stitch along the neck edge. Stitch the back of the body in the same manner.

Pin ears and arms to the right side of the front body section. (Diagram B, page 48.)

Pin the front and back body sections together, right sides facing (arms and ears will be inside).

Stitch together, leaving the bottom open. Clip corners and turn to the right side. Stuff firmly with polyester fiberfill, turn bottom edge under, and whipstitch closed. (If making the raccoon, insert the tail at the bottom edge and stitch in place as you close the opening.)

Cut larger facial features from felt. (Diagram A.) Glue in place and allow to dry. Remaining features can be embroidered or drawn in with embroidery pens or felt-tip markers.

For the dress: Cut 2 dress shapes for each doll. Fold pleats on each piece toward the center on the right side; stitch across to hold the pleats in place.

Sew the 2 dress pieces together, right sides facing, along the sides; stop at the openings for the arms. Make a narrow hem at the bottom.

Slip the dress over the doll and pull up to the neck. Fold the raw edges in at the arms. Tack the dress in place at the shoulders and along the front and back. Tack lace or ribbon trim around the neck (and hem, if desired).

continued

Raccoon   Koala Bear   Pig   Panda

Bear   Rabbit   Beaver   Monkey

𝒜   𝓑

For the duck and banana accessories, cut 2 pattern pieces for each from the same fabric. With right sides together, stitch around the entire edge. Make a small slit in the back and turn to the right side through the slit. Stuff firmly with polyester fiberfill and whipstitch slit closed.

For the carrot, cut the carrot and carrot top from fabric. Fold the carrot in half, right sides together, and stitch along the seam line, leaving the top open. Turn to the right side, stuff firmly, and gather at the top to close. Stitch top to carrot.

For the mortar board, cut a 1″ × 2″ strip of black felt; fold into a 1″ square. Close with a narrow zigzag stitch all around the edge. Stitch a piece of narrow gold ribbon to the center, and stitch mortar board to the doll head.

For the diploma, roll a 2″-long piece of white paper, and tie with a narrow piece of ribbon.

Design your own simply shaped accessories—trees, hearts, etc.—as you desire.

Hold the accessory firmly to the front of the dolls. Insert the needle through the back (under the dress) and pass it through to the front of the doll and through the accessory. Fold the arms in front of each doll and stitch the accessory and the ends of the arms in place. Pass the needle back through the doll and knot the thread in back under the dress.

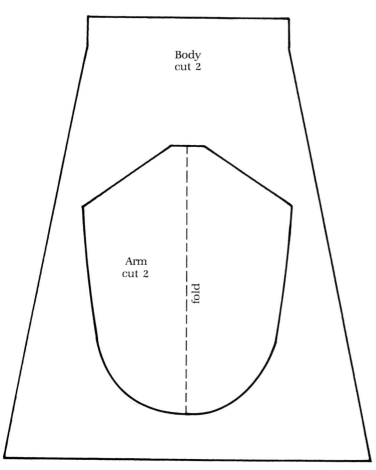

Body
cut 2

Arm
cut 2

fold

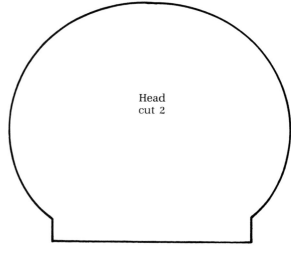

Head
cut 2

Carrot Top

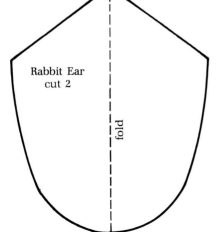

Banana

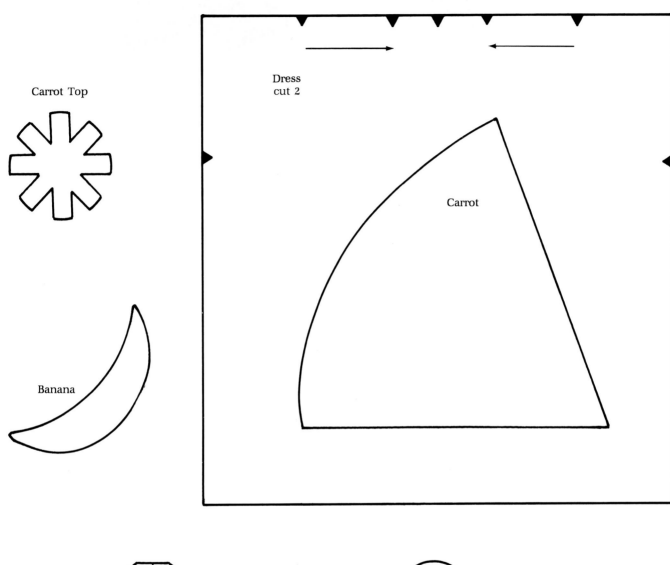

Dress
cut 2

Carrot

Rabbit Ear
cut 2

fold

Duck

49

Children's Workshop

Wrapping Paper Ornaments

Clever paper cutouts are a quiet afternoon activity for youngsters eager to participate in the holiday decorating. (They make a good classroom project as well!) This is also a great way to recycle scraps of wrapping paper and last year's cards. Simple designs will be easier to cut around than designs with complicated outlines.

MATERIALS:
  **scraps of wrapping paper or old
    Christmas cards
  poster board
  glue
  hole punch
  narrow ribbon**

Cover evenly a portion of the poster board with glue. (Spray adhesive works best, but it should be applied by an adult.) Carefully smooth the scrap of wrapping paper over the glue; allow to dry. Cut out the ornaments.

With a hole punch, make a small hole in the top of the design. Make a loop of narrow ribbon and hang the ornaments on the tree or tie onto packages as gift tags.

Coffee Can Planter

This project calls for help from mom or dad when it comes to cutting the molding to the right lengths, but the rest of the fun is for the children. For more vibrant results, the kids could paint the finished planter in bright Christmas colors. They may want to make several—one for mom, one for grandmother, and one for teacher!

MATERIALS:
  **10′ (½″) half-round molding
  1 pound size coffee can
  epoxy cement (the type that comes in a
    double tube applicator operated with a
    plunger so you don't have to mix the
    resin and catalyst)
  small piece each of 120 and 220 sandpaper**

Cut molding into 20 pieces, each 5½″ long. Using the seam in the can as a guide, glue the first piece of molding onto the can. Glue the remaining pieces around the can, butting them tightly against each other.

When the glue has set, sand the ends of the molding smooth with 120 paper. Remove any nicks or smudges on the sides of the planter with 220 sandpaper.

Felt Picture Frames

Children love to make their own gifts—and what could be more treasured than a photograph of the child in a handmade frame? These bright ideas make perfect presents for grandparents and parents alike.

MATERIALS:
   shirt cardboard
   felt in a variety of colors
   rubber cement
   photograph
   white glue
   ribbon, rickrack, or other trimmings

Cut a piece of felt ½" larger all the way around than the shirt cardboard. Spread rubber cement over the cardboard and over the piece of felt; allow to dry. Center and firmly press the felt to the cardboard.

Spread rubber cement over the back edges of the cardboard—½" all the way around. Fold the ½" excess felt over the edge of the cardboard and press smooth.

On a smaller piece of felt of a contrasting color, trace around the photograph to be used. Cut out a hole inside this traced line, leaving ¼" to ½" inside the line all around. (The hole can be square, rectangular, or even oval.) Use a small amount of glue to attach the two sides and the bottom edge of this piece to the felt-covered cardboard. Leave the top edge open so the picture can be slipped into the frame.

Trim the frame by glueing on felt cutouts of flowers or hearts, or use pieces of rickrack or ribbon.

Wraps & Cards

Tissue Paper Gift Sacks

Rainbow-colored tissue papers are easily transformed into fluffy bags to hide Santa's goodies. Use them in various sizes to wrap oversized gifts or to camouflage surprises with "give-away" shapes.

MATERIALS:
   tissue paper in bright colors (1 to 4 sheets, depending on size of gift bag)
   ½ to 1 yard ribbon or trim for drawstring

To prepare tissue paper for the desired gift bag size, use the following guidelines: 20″ × 30″ bag—4 sheets of tissue paper opened out flat and stacked together; 15″ × 20″ bag—2 sheets folded together in half; 10″ × 15″ bag—1 sheet folded in quarters; 7½″ × 10″ bag—½ sheet folded in quarters; 5″ × 7½″ bag—¼ sheet folded in quarters. Crease folds firmly.

To fold and sew casing, open out the 4 layers of folded tissue to a double layer of folded tissue. On one of the two longest sides of the rectangle, fold down a casing twice the width of ribbon or trim that is to be used as a drawstring. (The casing for the 20″ × 30″ bag is made by putting 2 sheets of paper together and folding equal casings on each pair along the 20″ side of the tissue.)

Sew down the casing close to the edge, using a medium zigzag stitch. Be careful not to catch the drawstring in the stitches.

To sew the sides of the bag, refold the bag to the desired size. Sew the 2 sides and the bottom, using a medium zigzag stitch. Begin the stitching on one side just below the casing and end the stitching on the opposite side just below the casing. Clip all threads. Use a warm, dry iron to press out any unwanted wrinkles.

Arrange the gift in the bag. Pull each side of the drawstring to close the bag. (Since the 20″ × 30″ bag is made in two pieces, you will have two sides with loose ends of the drawstring. Tie one side before pulling the other.)

Wine Bags

Even the most inexpensive wine becomes a fancy gift when it is presented in a glittering foil bag. This same ingenious wrap can be filled with unshelled pecans or walnuts or even stuffed with socks or scarves.

MATERIALS:
  foil wrapping paper
  brown wrapping paper
  1 yard cord or ribbon
  white glue
  hole punch

A

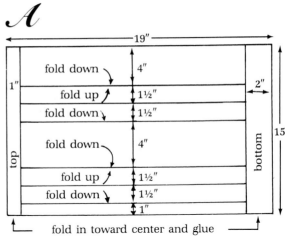

fold in toward center and glue

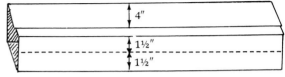

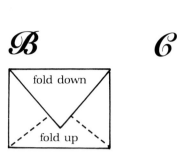

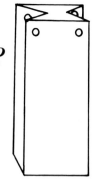

Cut both the foil and brown wrapping papers into 15″ × 19″ rectangles.

Thin the glue with a few drops of water. Apply the glue solution with a brush around the outside edges of the brown paper rectangle. Attach this piece to the wrong side of the foil paper rectangle. Allow the glue to dry completely.

With the foil side of the wrapping paper face down on a work surface, fold the paper rectangle according to Diagram A. First fold the top and bottom sections toward the center and glue in place. With the 4″ panel completely overlapping the 1″ panel, glue along the length of the bag to close the back. Fold the bottom of the bag and glue in place. (Diagram B.)

Pinch the front and back panels of the wine bag together; then punch a hole through all layers. (Diagram C.)

Insert the bottle of wine. Run a 1-yard cord or ribbon through the punched holes at the top of the bag and tie into a bow.

Christmas Seals

Make this year's gift wrapping your distinctive holiday signature with brightly colored seals cut from heavy wrapping paper. Use an original drawing, adapt a design from a Christmas card or paper, or trace around a cookie cutter. Because the seals are flat, they are ideal for decorating gifts that are to be boxed for mailing. This idea would also make striking, personalized Christmas cards and gift tags.

MATERIALS:
  several rolls of heavy wrapping paper
  lightweight cardboard or cookie cutters
  craft knife
  spray adhesive or rubber cement
  hole punch

If a cookie cutter is the source of your design, no cardboard pattern will be necessary. Just place the cookie cutter on wrapping paper and trace around it.

To make a pattern for other symbols, draw the designs onto cardboard and cut them out. Place the pattern on wrapping paper and trace around it. Cut out this shape; then cut a piece of paper to serve as its background.

With spray adhesive or rubber cement, glue the paper symbol to the background piece. You can make colored borders for the seal by glueing other slightly larger layers of paper to the back of the seal.

Wrap your gift in paper that matches or complements the seal; then glue the seal to the top of the wrapped package.

Fabric Boxes

What could be a more tempting Christmas gift than a batch of Candy Cane Cookies (recipe on page 85) presented in a beautiful fabric "box"? After the cookies have been eaten, the box may be used as a casserole cover for dressing up your entertaining all year long.

MATERIALS:

1 yard cotton or cotton/polyester fabric
1½ yards piping
2⅓ yards (¼"-wide) grosgrain ribbon
bonded polyester batting

Use your 13" × 9" × 2" casserole to determine the measurements of the fabric box. To make a pattern according to the diagram, first draw around the casserole for the bottom measurements. The height of the sides will be equal to the depth of the casserole (2") plus 1" for ease plus a ½" seam allowance. Extend the lines of the bottom to the sides to mark fold lines for the edges and points to attach the ribbon ties.

Using the outside measurements, cut 2 rectangles from the fabric and 1 from batting.

For the edging, cut a piece of piping equal to the measurement of the perimeter of the basket plus 1". Pin the piping to the right side of 1 piece of fabric (raw edges together) and machine baste along the ½" seam allowance.

Cut 8 (10") lengths of ribbon for the ties. Pin each length of ribbon to the right side of the fabric at points indicated on the diagram. The long ends should face the inside.

Place batting, then both pieces of fabric, right sides facing, together. Stitch along the previous basting lines, leaving 2" open to turn. Trim seams, turn, and hand sew the opening closed.

Tie the ribbons at each corner to pull up the edges around the casserole.

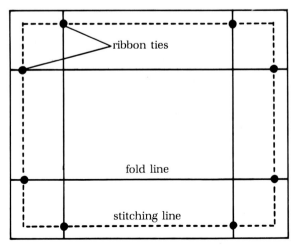

Handmade Christmas Cards

What could be more warmly received than saying "Merry Christmas" with cards and gift tags you design and decorate yourself? The instructions for the merry missives shown here are so simple, children can share in the excitement.

MATERIALS:

    scraps of gingham or calico fabrics
    white glue
    felt-tip markers in a variety of colors
    cards or paper
    construction paper

Purchase ready-made note cards with envelopes or make your own cards from construction paper to fit standard-sized envelopes.

"Holiday Greetings": Cut squares of fabric and glue around the edges of the card, forming a border. Print the message inside the frame in a bright color.

"Patchwork" cards and gift tags: Cut letters or shapes from calico fabric and glue to a colored card. The tree pattern is given here.

"Paper Cutouts": Cut snowflakes or bird design from paper and glue to white or brightly colored cards or gift tags. The bird pattern is given here.

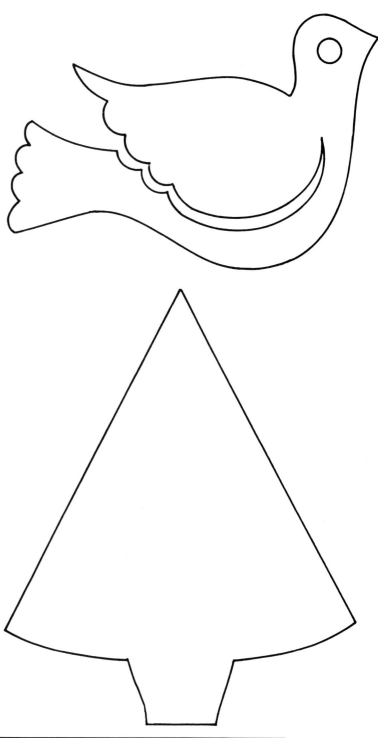

Mailing Tips

CARDS

As you are planning your Christmas cards, keep in mind the following regulations by the U.S. Postal Service. All envelopes must be rectangular in shape. Cards and envelopes smaller than 3½" × 5" cannot be mailed. Envelopes larger than 6⅛" × 11½", even if they weigh less than 1 ounce, require extra postage.

PACKAGES

Packages may be sent through the U.S. Postal Service by parcel post in weights up to 40 pounds (70 pounds for rural routes and small towns) and measurements of 84" of combined length and girth. "Priority" and "Express Mail" (at higher prices) can be used for packages up to 70 pounds in weight and up to 100" in combined length and girth. Refer to the chart for requirements of packaging, closing, and addressing.

United Parcel Service (UPS) accepts packages up to 50 pounds and up to 108" in combined length and girth. There is a pick-up fee for door-to-door service, but in peak periods, you may find it more convenient to take the package to UPS customer service.

CATEGORY	EXAMPLES	CONTAINER	CUSHIONING	CLOSURE
Soft Goods		Self-supporting box or tear-resistant bag		Reinforced tape or sealed bag
Liquids		Leak proof interior and secondary containers	Absorbent	Sealed with filament tape
Powders		Must be sift-proof		Sealed with filament tape
Perishables		Impermeable to content odor	Absorbent	Sealed with filament tape
Fragile Items		Fiberboard (minimum 175 lb test)	To distribute shocks and separate from container surfaces with foamed plastic or padding	Sealed and reinforced with filament tape
Awkward Loads		Fiberboard tubes and boxes with length not over 10 times girth	Pre-formed fiberboard or foamed plastic shapes	Tube ends equal to side wall strength

CONTAINER	CUSHIONING	CLOSURE		ADDRESSING
Fiberboard Manufacturer's Certificate 125 lb test to 20 lbs 175 lb test to 40 lbs 275 lb test to 70 lbs Paperboard up to 10 lbs	Wrap each item individually with enough padding to prevent damage from shock Separate wrapped items from outer package surfaces with padding or foamed plastic	CLOSURE	Pressure Sensitive Filament Tape is preferable to prevent accidental opening Reinforced Kraft Paper Tape Kraft Paper Tape	Address Labels should be readable from 30" away and should not be easily smeared or washed off Should contain ZIP Code Return Address should also be included inside of carton

Adapted from a U.S. Postal Service poster.

Celebrations from the Kitchen

What other time of the year brings such distinctive efforts from the kitchen? And what draws a family together more eagerly than a holiday table laden with the results of your efforts?

Southern families treasure—almost covet—the traditions of their recipes, particularly those dishes reserved for the family's Christmas dinner. For this reason, no menus or entrées are included here. Instead, "Celebrations from the Kitchen" offers over 75 specialties of the groaning board—the delicacies of the holiday season, the lagniappes of the family gatherings.

Throughout *Christmas with Southern Living*, you will find examples of food as presents. "Eleventh-Hour Gifts" suggests seasoned nuts, snack mixes, candies, or cookies to fill collectible tins. "Christmas Bazaar" offers patterns for a personalized cross-stitched lid to top off the jam or jelly creations, and a fabric "box" (that doubles as a casserole cover) to hold tempting Candy Cane Cookies.

The photographs within this chapter go on to suggest other ways to present your culinary talents. Debut a fruitcake in a serving basket and the recipient will be reminded of you whenever the basket is used later. Or, if you are giving a cake stand as a gift, top it with one of the special cakes or fruitcakes, and the gift is doubled.

Gifts of food are always welcome expressions of friendship and caring, and *Southern Living* recipes—all meticulously kitchen tested—are renowned for their quality and success at garnering compliments. Step-by-step instructions with photographs are offered for the more difficult preparations and for decorating our stunning gingerbread family. For a striking (and edible) table decoration, make gingerbread figures for each of the members of your family and use them as place markers when relatives gather for the holiday banquet.

Beverages

WHITFIELD EGGNOG

12 eggs, separated
1½ cups bourbon
¾ cup sugar, divided
1 pint whipping cream
1 tablespoon powdered sugar

Beat egg yolks until thick and lemon colored. Slowly add bourbon, beating constantly. Slowly add ½ cup sugar, a small amount at a time, beating until mixture is smooth; set aside.

Beat egg whites (at room temperature) until foamy. Gradually add remaining sugar, beating until stiff peaks form. Spoon beaten egg whites into chilled punch bowl. Beat whipping cream until foamy; add powdered sugar, and beat until soft peaks form. Spoon whipped cream on top of beaten egg whites. Pour egg yolk mixture over this and carefully fold all ingredients together. Yield: about 4½ quarts.

SUPERB BRANDY ALEXANDERS

½ gallon vanilla ice cream
½ cup brandy
¼ cup crème de cacao

Combine all ingredients in container of electric blender; blend well. Yield: about 1 quart.
Virginia Myers,
Lakeland, Florida.

KAHLÚA VELVET FROSTY

1 cup kahlúa or other coffee-flavored liqueur
1 pint vanilla ice cream
1 cup half-and-half
⅛ teaspoon almond extract
About 1½ cups crushed ice

Combine all ingredients in container of electric blender. Blend until smooth. Yield: about 1½ quarts.
Roger Tremblay,
Dallas, Texas.

OPEN-HOUSE PUNCH

2½ cups bourbon
1 (6-ounce) can frozen orange juice concentrate, thawed and undiluted
2 (6-ounce) cans frozen lemonade concentrate, thawed and undiluted
⅔ cup lemon juice
7 (10-ounce) bottles lemon-lime carbonated beverage, chilled
Lemon slices
Mint

Combine bourbon, orange juice, lemonade, and lemon juice; stir well. Add carbonated beverage and ice cubes. Garnish with lemon slices and mint. Yield: 3 quarts.
Edna Chadsey,
Corpus Christi, Texas.

CHAMPAGNE PUNCH

1 (25.4-ounce) bottle cold duck, chilled
1 (25.4-ounce) bottle pink champagne, chilled
4 cups cranberry juice, chilled
1 (33.8-ounce) bottle ginger ale, chilled

Combine all ingredients in a large punch bowl. Yield: about 3½ quarts.
Mrs. Denver Breeding,
Isom, Kentucky.

Whitfield Eggnog is so thick, rich, and creamy that it could be eaten with a spoon.

HOT BUTTERED RUM

1 pound butter, softened
1 (16-ounce) package light brown sugar
1 (16-ounce) package powdered sugar
2 teaspoons ground cinnamon
2 teaspoons ground nutmeg
1 quart vanilla ice cream, softened
  Light rum
  Whipped cream
  Cinnamon sticks

Combine butter, sugars, and spices; beat until light and fluffy. Add ice cream, stirring until well blended. Spoon mixture into a 2-quart freezer container; freeze.

To serve, thaw slightly. Place 3 tablespoons butter mixture and 1 jigger rum in a large mug; fill with boiling water. Stir well. (Any unused butter mixture can be refrozen.) Top with whipped cream, and serve with cinnamon stick stirrers. Yield: about 25 (8-ounce) servings.

Ginger Burch,
Waldorf, Maryland.

WASSAIL

4 cups pineapple juice
1½ cups apricot nectar
4 cups apple cider
1 cup orange juice
2 sticks cinnamon
2 teaspoons whole cloves
1 teaspoon ground nutmeg
  Bourbon to taste (optional)

Combine juices in a large saucepan. Tie spices in a cheesecloth bag; add to juice. Simmer mixture over medium heat for 30 minutes; remove spice bag. Add bourbon, if desired. Serve hot. Yield: 2½ quarts.

Mrs. Wayne B. Miles,
Chesterfield, Missouri.

HOT CRANBERRY TEA

4 cups fresh cranberries
3 quarts water
  Juice of 3 oranges, strained
  Juice of 3 lemons, strained
2 to 2½ cups sugar
1 stick cinnamon (optional)
1 teaspoon whole cloves (optional)

Combine cranberries and water in a large saucepan; bring to a boil. Reduce heat, and cook until berries pop. Remove from heat; cover and allow to cool completely. Strain cranberry juice, discarding pulp; add remaining ingredients to juice, and bring to a boil. Strain and serve hot. Yield: 3 quarts.

Mrs. Earl L. Faulkenberry,
Lancaster, South Carolina.

HOT MOCHA MIX

2 cups sugar
2 cups instant nonfat dry milk solids
2 cups nondairy creamer
1 cup cocoa
½ cup instant coffee powder

Combine all ingredients, and mix well. Store mix in an airtight container.

To serve, place 2 tablespoons mix in a cup. Add 1 cup boiling water, and stir well. Top with a marshmallow or whipped cream, if desired. Yield: enough for about 60 (8-ounce) servings.

Mrs. James F. Morgan,
High Point, North Carolina.

Breads

HONEY NUT LOAVES

½ cup butter or margarine, softened
1 cup honey
2 eggs
2 cups all-purpose flour
2 teaspoons baking powder
⅓ cup milk
1 cup chopped maraschino cherries
¼ cup chopped raisins
¼ cup chopped walnuts

Cream butter and honey; add eggs, one at a time, beating well after each addition.

Combine flour and baking powder; add to creamed mixture alternately with milk, beating well after each addition. Stir in cherries, raisins, and walnuts.

Spoon batter into 2 greased and floured 7½- × 3- × 2-inch loafpans. Bake at 350° for 40 to 50 minutes or until done. Yield: 2 loaves.

Note: Batter may be baked in 4 greased and floured miniature (4-inch) tube pans. Bake at 350° for 30 minutes or until done.

Mrs. Parke L. Cory,
Neosho, Missouri.

SWEDISH LIMPA

2 packages dry yeast
¼ cup warm water (105° to 115°)
2 cups rye flour
½ cup molasses
¼ cup firmly packed brown sugar
⅓ cup shortening
1 tablespoon salt
1 tablespoon caraway seeds
1 (4-ounce) package candied orange
   peel, chopped
3 cups hot water
2 tablespoons sugar
7 to 8 cups all-purpose flour
   Melted butter or margarine

Dissolve yeast in warm water. Combine rye flour, molasses, brown sugar, shortening, salt, caraway seeds, and orange peel in a large bowl. Add hot water, and mix well; cool to room temperature, and stir in yeast mixture and sugar. Gradually add flour, beating well after each addition.

Turn dough out on a floured surface; coat dough lightly with flour. Cover and let rest 15 minutes. Knead until smooth and elastic (about 8 to 10 minutes). Place dough in a well-greased bowl, turning to grease top. Cover and let rise in a warm place (85°), free from drafts, until doubled in bulk (about 45 minutes). Turn out on floured surface and knead until elastic.

Divide dough into quarters, and shape into round loaves. Place on greased baking sheets. Cover; let rise in a warm place, free from drafts, until doubled in bulk. Bake at 350° for 40 minutes. Brush hot loaves with melted butter. Cool on wire racks. Yield: 4 loaves.

Note: Bread may also be baked in 2 (9- × 5- × 3-inch) and 2 (8- × 4- × 3-inch) loafpans.

Mrs. Richard Merrill,
Relay, Maryland.

ALMOND SWIRL RING

1 cup milk
6 tablespoons butter or margarine
⅓ cup sugar
½ teaspoon salt
3 to 4 cups all-purpose flour, divided
1 package dry yeast
1 egg, beaten
⅓ cup sugar
2 tablespoons butter or margarine, softened
½ cup ground almonds
¼ teaspoon almond extract
1 cup powdered sugar
2 to 3 tablespoons milk or water
Candied cherry halves
Whole blanched almonds, toasted

Combine first 4 ingredients in a small saucepan; heat just until warm (about 115°). Combine 2 cups flour with yeast; add warm milk mixture and egg. Beat well. Stir in enough remaining flour to make a soft dough.

Turn dough out on a floured surface, and knead 3 to 5 minutes; shape into a ball. Place in a greased bowl, turning to grease top. Cover; let rise in a warm place (85°), free from drafts, until doubled in bulk (about 1 hour). Punch dough down, and let rise 10 additional minutes.

Place dough on a floured surface, and roll into an 18- × 12-inch rectangle. Combine ⅓ cup sugar, 2 tablespoons butter, ground almonds, and almond extract; blend well, and spread over dough. Starting with long edge, roll dough up jellyroll fashion; pinch edges together to seal.

Place roll on a greased cookie sheet; shape into a ring, and pinch ends together to seal. Using kitchen shears or a sharp knife, make a cut every inch around ring (cut should go two-thirds of way through roll). Gently pull slices out and

twist, overlapping slices slightly. Cover; let rise in warm place, free from drafts, until doubled in bulk (about 45 minutes).

Bake at 375° for 20 to 25 minutes. Combine powdered sugar and 2 to 3 tablespoons milk to make a glaze; drizzle over hot ring. Garnish with candied cherries and almonds. Yield: 16 to 20 servings.

Debbie Hill,
Charlotte, North Carolina.

CREAM CHEESE BRAIDS

1 cup commercial sour cream
½ cup sugar
1 teaspoon salt
½ cup butter or margarine, melted
2 packages dry yeast
½ cup warm water (105° to 115°)
2 eggs, beaten
4 cups all-purpose flour
Cream Cheese Filling
Glaze (recipe follows)

Heat sour cream over low heat; stir in sugar, salt, and butter; cool to lukewarm. Sprinkle yeast over warm water in large mixing bowl, stirring until yeast dissolves. Add sour cream mixture, eggs, and flour; mix well. Cover tightly; refrigerate overnight.

The next day, divide dough into four equal parts; roll out each part on a well-floured board into a 12- × 8-inch rectangle. Spread one-fourth of Cream Cheese Filling on each rectangle; roll up jellyroll fashion, beginning at long sides. Pinch edges together, and fold ends under slightly; place rolls seam side down on greased baking sheets.

Slit each roll at 2-inch intervals about two-thirds of way through dough to resemble a braid. Cover and let rise in a warm place, free from drafts, until doubled in bulk (about 1 hour). Bake at 375° for 12 to 15 minutes. Spread with glaze while warm. Yield: 4 (12-inch) loaves.

Cream Cheese Filling:

- 2 (8-ounce) packages cream cheese, softened
- ¾ cup sugar
- 1 egg, beaten
- ⅛ teaspoon salt
- 2 teaspoons vanilla extract

Combine cream cheese and sugar in a small mixing bowl. Add egg, salt, and vanilla; mix well. Yield: about 2 cups.

Glaze:

- 2 cups powdered sugar
- ¼ cup milk
- 2 teaspoons vanilla extract

Combine all ingredients in a small bowl; mix well. Yield: about 1 cup.   *Phyllis Cannon, Stanley, North Carolina.*

OLD-FASHIONED CHRISTMAS BREAD

- 2 packages dry yeast
- ¼ cup warm water (105° to 115°)
- 1 cup milk
- ⅓ cup butter or margarine
- ¼ cup sugar
- ½ teaspoon salt
- 1 teaspoon vanilla extract
- 1 egg
- 3½ cups all-purpose flour, divided
  Fruit-Nut Filling
- 1 egg
- 1 teaspoon water
- ½ cup slivered almonds

Dissolve yeast in warm water, stirring well; set aside.

Scald milk; pour over butter, sugar, and salt in a large bowl, and stir until butter melts. Cool to 105° to 115°. Add yeast mixture, vanilla, egg, and 2½ cups flour, stirring until smooth. Gradually add remainder of flour, stirring until a stiff dough is formed. Turn dough out on a floured surface; knead until smooth and elastic (about 5 minutes).

Place dough in a greased bowl, turning to grease top. Cover and let rise in a warm place (85°), free of drafts, about 45 minutes or until doubled in bulk. Turn onto a lightly floured surface, and knead 10 times.

Roll into a 20- × 12-inch rectangle. Spread Fruit-Nut Filling evenly over dough, leaving a 1-inch margin. Roll up lengthwise; seal, and place seam side down on a greased cookie sheet. Shape into a horseshoe. Cover and let rise in a warm place (85°), free of drafts, 1 hour or until doubled in bulk.

Combine egg and water, beating until frothy; brush over surface of dough; sprinkle with almonds. Bake at 375° for 25 to 30 minutes. Remove from cookie sheet, and cool on a wire rack. Yield: 1 loaf.

Fruit-Nut Filling:

- ¼ cup sugar
- 2 tablespoons butter or margarine, softened
- ½ teaspoon ground cinnamon
- 1 cup raisins
- ½ cup candied red cherries
- ½ cup candied green cherries
- ¼ cup slivered blanched almonds

Combine all ingredients, and mix well. Yield: enough filling for 1 loaf.   *Linda Whitt, Missouri City, Texas.*

STOLLEN

1 package dry yeast
¼ cup warm water (105° to 115°)
½ cup shortening
2 tablespoons sugar
1½ teaspoons salt
2 eggs
1 cup milk, scalded and cooled to lukewarm
4 to 5 cups all-purpose flour
1 cup diced mixed candied fruits, divided
1 cup raisins, divided
1 cup powdered sugar
1½ tablespoons hot water
   Sliced almonds (optional)
   Chopped candied fruits (optional)

Combine yeast and water in a small bowl; let mixture stand 5 minutes.

In a large bowl, cream shortening, sugar, and salt until fluffy. Add eggs, one at a time, beating well after each addition. Stir in milk and yeast mixture. Add flour, 1 cup at a time, stirring well, until a soft dough is formed. Cover tightly, and let rise in a warm place (85°), free of drafts, 1½ hours or until doubled in bulk.

Punch dough down; divide in half, and set one half aside. Knead ½ cup candied fruits and ½ cup raisins into dough on a floured surface. Roll to a 10-inch circle; fold in half, and place on a greased baking sheet. Let rise in a warm place (85°), free of drafts, 30 minutes or until doubled in bulk.

Repeat kneading, rolling, and rising process with remaining dough. Bake at 375° for 25 to 30 minutes or until golden brown; loaves will sound hollow when tapped on top with finger. Cool on wire racks 2 to 3 minutes.

Combine powdered sugar and hot water; spread over each loaf. Garnish with sliced almonds and chopped candied fruits, if desired. Yield: 2 loaves.   *Evelyn Farrow,*
New Bern, North Carolina.

Holiday sweet breads highlight a Southern Christmas: Danish Pastry Wreath (foreground), Stollen, and Old-Fashioned Christmas Bread.

DANISH PASTRY WREATH

1½ cups butter or margarine, softened
¼ cup all-purpose flour
¾ cup milk
⅓ cup sugar
1 teaspoon salt
2 packages dry yeast
½ cup warm water (105° to 115°)
1 egg
    About 3¾ cups all-purpose flour
    Almond Filling
    Glaze (recipe follows)
    Candied cherries (optional)

Beat butter and ¼ cup flour until smooth and fluffy. Place waxed paper on a large, wet baking sheet. On the baking sheet, spread butter mixture evenly into a 12- × 8-inch rectangle. Chill well.

Scald milk; add sugar and salt, stirring until sugar dissolves. Cool to lukewarm (105° to 115°).

Combine yeast and water in a large bowl; let stand 5 minutes. Stir in milk, egg, and 3¾ cups flour; beat until mixture is smooth and leaves side of bowl (dough will be soft). Cover and chill 30 minutes.

Turn dough out onto a floured surface. Place stockinette cover on rolling pin; flour well. Roll dough to a 12- × 16-inch rectangle. Fit cold butter mixture over half of dough, leaving a margin at edges; remove waxed paper. Fold dough over butter; pinch edges to seal.

Place fold of dough to the right; roll dough to a 16- × 8-inch rectangle. (If butter breaks through dough, flour heavily and continue rolling.) Fold rectangle into thirds; pinch edges to seal. Wrap dough in waxed paper; chill 1 hour. Repeat rolling, folding, and sealing process; chill 30 minutes. Repeat rolling, folding, and sealing process; wrap dough in aluminum foil, and chill 8 hours.

Divide dough into 2 equal portions; chill half of dough. Roll remaining dough into a 22- × 8-inch rectangle. Cut dough into 3 equal lengthwise strips. Spread ⅓ cup Almond Filling down center of each strip, leaving a 1-inch margin at each end.

Close edges of dough over filling, pinching edges and ends to seal; turn ropes seam side down. Firmly pinch ends of the three ropes together at one end to seal. Braid ropes together; firmly pinch ends together to seal.

Place brown paper on a baking sheet. Carefully transfer braid to baking sheet; form into a wreath with a 6-inch-diameter hole. Join ends of braid; firmly pinch ends to seal.

Cover; let rise in a warm place (85°), free of drafts, until doubled in bulk. Bake at 375° for 30 minutes or until golden brown. Carefully transfer to wire rack to cool (pastry is very fragile, so move gently).

Repeat process with remaining dough. Spread half of glaze over each wreath. Garnish each with candied cherries, if desired. Yield: 2 coffee cakes.

Almond Filling:

¾ cup zwieback crumbs
½ cup melted butter
1 egg, beaten
½ teaspoon almond extract
1 (8-ounce) can almond paste

Combine zwieback crumbs, butter, egg, and almond extract; stir well. Cut almond paste into crumb mixture with a pastry blender until well blended. Yield: about 2 cups.

Glaze:

3 to 4 tablespoons milk
2 cups powdered sugar

Stir milk into powdered sugar until smooth. Yield: glaze for 2 coffee cakes.

Sue-Sue Hartstern,
Louisville, Kentucky.

BRAIDED LIGHTBREAD

3 cups warm water (105° to 115°),
    divided
2 packages dry yeast
1 tablespoon plus 1 teaspoon sugar
10 cups all-purpose flour, divided
1 tablespoon plus 1 teaspoon salt
2 eggs, slightly beaten
3 tablespoons vegetable oil
1 egg yolk, beaten
1 teaspoon water
    Sesame or poppy seeds (optional)

Combine 2 cups water, yeast, and sugar in a
small bowl; set aside to rise. Combine 9 cups
flour, salt, eggs, and oil in a large mixing bowl.
Add yeast mixture and 1 cup water; mix well.

Sprinkle remaining 1 cup flour on pastry cloth
or board. Turn out dough and knead until
smooth and elastic (about 8 to 10 minutes). Place
in a greased bowl, turning to grease top. Cover
and let rise in a warm place (85°), free from
drafts, until doubled in bulk.

Turn dough out on floured surface; punch
down and divide in half. Divide each half into 3
equal parts, and form into 15-inch lengths. Place
3 lengths on a greased baking sheet and braid.
Repeat with remaining 3 lengths. Press ends of
each braid together, and turn under firmly.
Cover and let rise until doubled in bulk (about 45
minutes).

Combine egg yolk and water; brush top of
braids. Sprinkle with sesame seeds, if desired.
Bake at 350° for 45 minutes. Cool on wire racks.
Yield: 2 loaves. *Mrs. Sam Huddleston,*
Brownsville, Texas.

RAISIN CINNAMON-SWIRL BREAD

1 cup raisins
1⅓ cups milk, divided
1 package dry yeast
½ cup sugar
1 egg, beaten
¼ teaspoon salt
½ cup butter or margarine, melted
1 teaspoon ground cardamom
4 cups all-purpose flour
2 tablespoons sugar
2 tablespoons ground cinnamon
1 egg white, lightly beaten

Cover raisins with water and soak until plump.
Scald ⅓ cup milk; cool to 105° to 115°. Sprinkle
yeast in milk, and stir until yeast is dissolved.
Combine remaining 1 cup milk, ½ cup sugar,
egg, salt, and butter in a large bowl; mix well. Stir
in yeast mixture. Combine cardamom and flour;
gradually add to milk mixture, stirring until a
soft dough forms.

Turn dough out on a lightly floured board;
knead until smooth and elastic. Place in a
greased bowl, turning to grease top. Cover and
let rise in a warm place (85°), free from drafts,
until doubled in bulk (about 1 hour).

Punch dough down; place on a lightly floured
board, and roll into a 14- × 12-inch rectangle.
Combine 2 tablespoons sugar and cinnamon;
sprinkle over dough. Drain raisins, and sprinkle
over cinnamon mixture. Roll up jellyroll fashion.

Place roll on a greased baking sheet, seam side
down. Cover and let rise in a warm place 35
minutes. Brush dough with egg white. Using a
sharp knife, slash top of dough at 2-inch intervals. Bake at 350° for 30 to 40 minutes or until loaf
sounds hollow when tapped. Yield: 1 loaf.
Mrs. Harvey Kidd,
Hernando, Mississippi.

Christmas is a time for giving and sharing.
(Clockwise from top left) German Chocolate Fudge,
Cheese Crock, Swedish Nuts, Homemade Granola,
Pecan Snacks, Orange Butter, Brandied Pear Sauce,
and Raisin Cinnamon-Swirl Bread.

Cakes & Fruitcakes

COCONUT-SOUR CREAM LAYER CAKE

1 (18½-ounce) package butter-flavored cake mix
2 cups sugar
1 (16-ounce) carton commercial sour cream
1 (12-ounce) package frozen coconut, thawed
1½ cups frozen whipped topping, thawed

Prepare cake mix according to package directions, making two 8-inch layers; when completely cool, split both layers horizontally.

Combine sugar, sour cream, and coconut, blending well; chill. Reserve 1 cup sour cream mixture for frosting; spread remainder between layers of cake.

Combine reserved sour cream mixture with whipped topping; blend until smooth. Spread on top and sides of cake. Seal cake in an airtight container, and refrigerate for 3 days before serving. Yield: one 8-inch layer cake.

Mrs. Thomas R. Cherry,
Birmingham, Alabama.

HUMMINGBIRD CAKE

3 cups all-purpose flour
2 cups sugar
1 teaspoon salt
1 teaspoon soda
1 teaspoon ground cinnamon
3 eggs, beaten
1½ cups vegetable oil
1½ teaspoons vanilla extract
1 (8-ounce) can crushed pineapple, undrained
2 cups chopped pecans or walnuts, divided
2 cups chopped bananas
Cream cheese frosting (recipe follows)

Combine dry ingredients in a large mixing bowl; add eggs and oil, stirring until dry ingredients are moistened. Do not beat. Stir in vanilla, pineapple, 1 cup chopped pecans, and bananas.

Spoon batter into 3 well-greased and floured 9-inch cakepans. Bake at 350° for 25 to 30 minutes or until cake tests done. Cool in pans 10 minutes; remove from pans, and cool completely.

Spread frosting between layers and on top and sides of cake. Sprinkle with remaining pecans. Yield: one 3-layer cake.

Cream Cheese Frosting:

1 (8-ounce) package cream cheese, softened
½ cup butter or margarine, softened
1 (16-ounce) package powdered sugar
1 teaspoon vanilla extract

Combine cream cheese and butter; cream until smooth. Add powdered sugar, beating until light and fluffy. Stir in vanilla. Yield: enough for a 3-layer cake.
Mrs. L. H. Wiggins,
Greensboro, North Carolina.

HOLIDAY COCONUT CAKE

⅓ cup shortening
⅓ cup butter, softened
1¾ cups sugar
3 cups cake flour
3½ teaspoons baking powder
¾ teaspoon salt
1⅓ cups milk
2 teaspoons vanilla extract
4 egg whites
  Lemon filling (recipe follows)
  Fluffy Frosting
  Freshly grated coconut

Cream shortening, butter, and sugar until light and fluffy. Sift together flour, baking powder, and salt; add to creamed mixture alternately with milk, beating well after each addition. Stir in vanilla. Beat egg whites until stiff, and fold into batter.

Pour batter into 3 greased and floured 9-inch cakepans; bake at 350° for 25 minutes or until a wooden pick inserted in center comes out clean. Cool in pans 10 minutes. Remove from pans and complete cooling on wire racks. Spread lemon filling between layers. Frost top and sides of cake with Fluffy Frosting, and sprinkle with coconut. Yield: one 3-layer cake.

Lemon Filling:

1 cup plus 2 tablespoons sugar
¼ cup cornstarch
1 cup plus 2 tablespoons water
2 egg yolks, slightly beaten
2 tablespoons butter
3 tablespoons lemon juice
1 tablespoon grated lemon rind

Combine sugar and cornstarch in a saucepan; gradually stir in water. Cook over medium heat, stirring constantly, until mixture thickens and boils. Boil 1 minute.

Slowly stir about one-fourth of the hot mixture into egg yolks; add to remaining hot mixture in saucepan. Boil 1 minute longer, stirring constantly. Remove from heat and continue stirring until smooth. Stir in butter, lemon juice, and rind. Cool. Yield: about 2 cups.

Fluffy Frosting:

1 cup sugar
⅓ cup water
¼ teaspoon cream of tartar
2 egg whites
½ teaspoon vanilla extract
½ teaspoon almond extract

Combine sugar, water, and cream of tartar in a heavy saucepan. Cook over low heat without stirring until syrup spins a 6- to 8-inch thread.

Beat egg whites until soft peaks form. Continue to beat egg whites, and slowly pour in syrup mixture. Add flavorings; beat well. Yield: enough for one 3-layer cake.

Mrs. Walter Wickstrom,
Pelham, Alabama.

EGGNOG CAKE

1 cup butter or margarine, softened
2 cups powdered sugar, sifted
5 egg yolks
¼ cup brandy
1 cup slivered almonds, toasted and divided
1 (10-ounce) commercial angel food cake
1 cup whipping cream, whipped

Cream butter and sugar until light and fluffy. Add egg yolks, one at a time, beating well after each addition. Stir in brandy and ¾ cup almonds.

Slice cake horizontally into four layers; spread creamed mixture between layers. Chill 24 hours. Just before serving, spread whipped cream on top and sides of cake; sprinkle with remaining almonds. Yield: one 4-layer cake.

Eleanor Brandt,
Arlington, Texas.

PEACH BRANDY POUND CAKE

1 cup butter or margarine, softened
3 cups sugar
6 eggs
3 cups all-purpose flour
¼ teaspoon soda
Pinch of salt
1 cup commercial sour cream
2 teaspoons rum
1 teaspoon orange extract
¼ teaspoon almond extract
½ teaspoon lemon extract
1 teaspoon vanilla extract
½ cup peach brandy

Cream butter; gradually add sugar, beating well. Add eggs, one at a time, mixing well after each addition. Combine dry ingredients; add to creamed mixture alternately with sour cream, beating well after each addition. Stir in remaining ingredients.

Pour batter into a well-greased and floured 10-inch Bundt pan or tube pan. Bake at 325° for 1 hour and 20 minutes or until cake tests done. Yield: one 10-inch cake. *Patricia Morrison, Honolulu, Hawaii.*

STEAMED HOLIDAY PUDDING

1 cup chopped dates
½ cup chopped pecans or black walnuts
2 cups all-purpose flour, divided
1 cup sugar
1 teaspoon soda
1 teaspoon baking powder
1 egg, beaten
1 cup milk
1½ teaspoons lemon juice
¼ teaspoon grated lemon rind
Lemon slices
Lemon sauce (recipe follows)

Coat dates and pecans with about 2 tablespoons flour; set aside.

Combine remaining flour, sugar, soda, and baking powder; add egg and milk, stirring until dry ingredients are moistened. Stir in date mixture, lemon juice, and lemon rind.

Pour batter into a well-greased 1½-quart pudding mold, and cover tightly with lid. Or pour batter into a well-greased heatproof bowl, and cover with a double thickness of buttered aluminum foil; secure foil with string.

Place mold on rack in a large kettle; add boiling water, filling kettle one-third full. Cover and steam 2 to 2½ hours. (Water should boil gently; add more water as needed.)

Remove mold from kettle; remove lid from mold to allow steam to escape. Loosen pudding from sides of mold, and invert onto serving dish. Garnish with lemon slices, and serve hot or cold with lemon sauce. Wrap leftovers tightly in foil, and store in refrigerator. Yield: 8 to 10 servings.

Lemon Sauce:

1 cup sugar
1 tablespoon cornstarch
1 cup boiling water
2 tablespoons butter or margarine
¼ teaspoon grated lemon rind
1½ teaspoons lemon juice
Rum or brandy to taste (optional)

Combine sugar and cornstarch in a saucepan; gradually add water, stirring constantly until smooth. Add butter, lemon rind, and lemon juice. Bring to a boil, and boil until thickened; stir constantly. Add rum, if desired. Serve hot or cold. Yield: 1¼ cups.

KENTUCKY BOURBON CAKE

  2 cups sugar
1½ cups butter, softened
  6 eggs
½ cup molasses
  4 cups all-purpose flour
2½ teaspoons baking powder
  2 teaspoons ground nutmeg
  1 (15-ounce) package raisins
  1 cup chopped candied pineapple
  1 cup chopped candied cherries
  1 cup orange marmalade
  2 pounds chopped pecans (about 8
      cups)
  1 cup bourbon
    Additional candied cherries (optional)

Cream sugar and butter until light and fluffy; add eggs, one at a time, beating well after each addition. Add molasses, and mix well.

Combine flour, baking powder, and nutmeg; set aside. Combine fruits, marmalade, and pecans in a large bowl; add 1 cup flour mixture and toss to coat fruit. Add remainder of flour mixture to creamed mixture alternately with bourbon; mix well. Stir in fruit and pecans.

Grease one 10-inch tube pan or two 9- × 5- × 3-inch loafpans; line with greased heavy brown paper. (Do not use recycled paper.) Spoon batter into pan, and cover with greased brown paper. Bake at 250° for 2½ to 3 hours or until done. Do not overcook. Cool completely. Garnish with additional candied cherries, if desired.

Wrap cake in a cloth that has been soaked in bourbon; place in a container and seal, or wrap in aluminum foil. Yield: one 10-inch cake or two loaves.

Note: The secret is to wrap it in a bourbon-soaked cloth and let it ripen—a month is not too long. Refrigerate for easier slicing.

MINIATURE WHITE FRUITCAKES

¾ cup butter or margarine, softened
  1 cup sugar
  5 eggs
  2 cups all-purpose flour
  1 teaspoon cream of tartar
¼ teaspoon salt
½ teaspoon soda
½ pound red and green candied
      cherries, chopped (about 1¼ cups)
½ pound yellow and green candied
      pineapple, chopped (about 1¼ cups)
½ pound mixed candied fruit and peel,
      chopped (about 1¼ cups)
½ pound golden raisins (about 1½ cups)
  2 cups fresh or frozen shredded
      coconut
  2 cups chopped pecans
    Additional candied fruit and pecans
    (optional)

Cream butter and sugar until light and fluffy. Add eggs, one at a time, beating well after each addition. Combine dry ingredients. Combine fruit and pecans in a large bowl; add about 1 cup dry ingredients, mixing well. Add remainder of dry ingredients to creamed mixture, and mix well; then stir in fruit mixture.

Spoon batter into well-greased miniature Bundt pans or loafpans, filling about three-fourths full. Bake at 350° for 20 to 25 minutes or until done. Cool; decorate with additional candied fruit and pecans, if desired. Yield: 8 to 10 miniature fruitcakes.   *Jerre R. Lett,*
Newton, North Carolina.

Light Fruitcake and Miniature White Fruitcakes are cleverly packaged in handsome gift baskets.

LIGHT FRUITCAKE

- 1½ cups butter, softened
- 1½ cups sugar
- 1 tablespoon vanilla extract
- 1 tablespoon lemon extract
- 7 eggs, separated and at room temperature
- 3 cups all-purpose flour
- 1½ pounds candied yellow, green, and red pineapple (about 3 cups)
- 1 pound candied red and green cherries (about 2 cups)
- ¼ pound candied citron (about ½ cup)
- ½ pound golden raisins (about 1½ cups)
- 3 cups pecan halves
- 1 cup black walnuts, coarsely chopped
- ½ cup all-purpose flour
  Additional candied fruit and nuts (optional)
- ¼ cup brandy
  Additional brandy

Make a liner for a 10-inch tube pan by drawing a circle with an 18-inch diameter on a piece of brown paper. (Do not use recycled paper.) Cut out circle; set pan in center, and draw around base of pan and inside tube. Fold circle into eighths, having the drawn lines on the outside.

Cut off tip end of circle along inside drawn line. Unfold paper; cut along folds to the outside drawn line. From another piece of brown paper, cut another circle with a 10-inch diameter; grease and set aside. Place the 18-inch liner in pan; grease and set aside.

Cream butter and sugar until light and fluffy. Stir in flavorings. Beat egg yolks. Alternately add egg yolks and 3 cups flour to creamed mixture.

Combine candied fruit, raisins, and nuts in a large mixing bowl; dredge with ½ cup flour, stirring to coat well. Stir mixture into batter. Beat egg whites until stiff; then fold into batter.

Spoon batter into prepared pan. Arrange additional fruit and nuts on top, if desired. Cover pan with greased 10-inch brown paper circle. Bake at 250° for 2½ to 3 hours or until cake tests done. Remove from oven. Take off paper cover, and slowly pour ¼ cup brandy evenly over cake; cool on rack.

74

Remove cake from pan; peel paper liner from cake. Wrap cake in brandy-soaked cheesecloth or clothlike disposable wiper. Store in an airtight container in a cool place 3 weeks. Pour a small amount of brandy over cake each week. Yield: one 10-inch cake.

Note: Cake may be baked in four 9- × 5- × 3-inch paper-lined loafpans. Bake at 250° for 1½ hours or until done.　　*Mrs. Robert L. Perry, Richmond, Virginia.*

STEPS TO A PERFECT FRUITCAKE

C Combine fruit, raisins, and nuts in a large bowl; dredge with ½ cup flour.

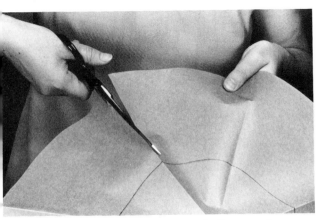

A Cut a circle with an 18-inch diameter from brown paper. Fit liner into a 10-inch pan, covering bottom and sides; grease paper. Cut another 10-inch circle; grease.

D Stir fruit mixture into batter; fold in stiffly beaten egg whites. Spoon batter into prepared pan; cover with 10-inch paper circle. Bake as directed.

B Cream butter and sugar; add flavorings. Add egg yolks alternately with flour to creamed mixture.

E Pour brandy over cake, and let cool; then remove from pan. Peel paper liner from cake.

75

HOLIDAY LOG CAKE

¾ teaspoon baking powder
¼ teaspoon salt
4 eggs
¾ cup sugar
¾ cup all-purpose flour
¼ cup cocoa
1 teaspoon vanilla extract
2 to 3 tablespoons powdered sugar
2 cups sweetened whipped cream
3 (1-ounce) squares unsweetened chocolate
¼ cup butter or margarine
1 tablespoon instant coffee granules
Dash of salt
⅓ cup boiling water
About 2½ cups sifted powdered sugar
Candied cherries

Grease a 15- × 10- × 1-inch jellyroll pan; line with waxed paper and grease lightly. Set aside.

Combine baking powder, ¼ teaspoon salt, and eggs (at room temperature) in mixing bowl; beat at medium speed of electric mixer until blended. Add sugar gradually, beating until thick and light colored. Fold in flour, cocoa, and vanilla.

Spread mixture evenly into prepared pan. Bake at 400° for 13 minutes or until surface springs back when gently pressed.

Sift 2 to 3 tablespoons powdered sugar in a 15- × 10-inch rectangle on a linen towel. Turn cake out on sugar; remove waxed paper from cake. Trim crisp edges, if necessary. Starting with short end, carefully roll cake and towel, jellyroll fashion. Cool thoroughly on wire rack. Unroll; spread with whipped cream, and reroll. Chill.

Melt chocolate in top of a double boiler; blend in butter, coffee, dash of salt, and boiling water, stirring until smooth. Cool to lukewarm. Stir in about 2½ cups powdered sugar to make a spreading consistency. Spread frosting evenly over cake. Mark with tines of a fork to resemble bark of a tree. Decorate with candied cherries. Refrigerate until serving time. Yield: 8 to 10 servings.
Claudia Hibbard,
Tuscaloosa, Alabama.

VELVETY CHOCOLATE CAKE

½ cup buttermilk
1 teaspoon soda
2 cups all-purpose flour
2 cups sugar
¼ teaspoon salt
½ cup butter or margarine
1 cup water
¼ cup cocoa
2 eggs, beaten
Velvety Chocolate Frosting

Combine buttermilk and soda; set aside. Combine flour, sugar, and salt in a mixing bowl.

Combine butter, water, and cocoa in a saucepan; bring to a boil. Pour over flour mixture, and mix well; cool. Add eggs and buttermilk mixture; mix well.

Pour into 2 greased and floured 8-inch round cakepans. Bake at 350° for 25 to 30 minutes or until cake tests done. Cool in pans 10 minutes; remove from pans and complete cooling on wire racks. Frost with Velvety Chocolate Frosting. Yield: one 2-layer cake.

Velvety Chocolate Frosting:

½ cup butter or margarine
¼ cup plus 2 tablespoons milk
¼ cup cocoa
1 (16-ounce) package powdered sugar

Combine butter, milk, and cocoa in a saucepan; bring to a boil. Remove from heat; add powdered sugar, stirring well. Spread warm frosting on cake. Yield: enough for one 8-inch layer cake.
Penny Franks,
Birmingham, Alabama.

So rich, so moist—Velvety Chocolate Cake is a recipe you'll treasure long after the holiday season is past.

BELGIAN MOCHA CAKE

2½ cups sugar, divided
3 tablespoons water
2 (1-ounce) squares unsweetened
    chocolate
¾ cup butter or margarine, softened
1 teaspoon vanilla extract
4 eggs, separated
2¼ cups sifted cake flour
½ teaspoon soda
½ teaspoon salt
1 cup milk
1 teaspoon cream of tartar
    Mocha frosting (recipe follows)
    Grated chocolate (optional)

Combine ½ cup sugar, water, and chocolate in a heavy saucepan; place over low heat, stirring until chocolate is melted. Remove from heat; cool.

Cream butter; gradually add remaining 2 cups sugar, beating well. Stir in vanilla. Add egg yolks, one at a time, beating well after each addition. Stir in chocolate mixture.

Combine flour, soda, and salt; add to creamed mixture alternately with milk, beating well after each addition. Beat egg whites until frothy; add cream of tartar, and beat until stiff peaks form. Fold into batter.

Grease three 9-inch or four 8-inch round cake-pans; line with greased waxed paper, and dust with flour. Pour batter into prepared pans, and bake at 350° for 25 to 30 minutes. Cool in pans 10 minutes; remove from pans and cool completely on wire racks. Spread mocha frosting between layers and on top and sides of cake. Store in refrigerator; may be frozen. If desired, garnish with grated chocolate before serving. Yield: one 3- or 4-layer cake.

Mocha Frosting:

1 cup butter, softened
2 to 2¼ cups powdered sugar, divided
1 tablespoon instant coffee powder
¾ teaspoon cocoa
¾ teaspoon hot water
2 egg yolks
1 to 1½ tablespoons almond extract
2 tablespoons rum

Cream butter and 1½ cups powdered sugar until light and fluffy. Combine coffee, cocoa, and water; stir into creamed mixture. Add egg yolks, and beat 5 minutes. Stir in almond extract and rum. Add enough of remaining sugar to make spreading consistency (frosting gets quite firm when refrigerated). Yield: enough for one 3- or 4-layer cake.

Anita Cochran,
Nashville, Tennessee.

TIPSY CAKE

6 eggs, separated
1½ cups sugar, divided
1 teaspoon vanilla extract
1½ cups all-purpose flour
1½ teaspoons baking powder
½ teaspoon salt
4½ tablespoons cold water
2 cups sherry
1 cup apple jelly, divided
1¼ cups sliced almonds, toasted
    Custard (recipe follows)
    Whipped cream frosting (recipe
    follows)

Beat egg yolks until light; gradually add ¾ cup sugar, beating until thick and lemon colored. Add vanilla.

Combine flour, baking powder, and salt; add to egg mixture alternately with water, mixing well.

Beat egg whites until foamy; gradually add remaining ¾ cup sugar, beating until stiff peaks form. Fold egg whites into cake batter until thoroughly mixed.

Pour cake batter slowly into an ungreased 10-inch tube pan; bake at 350° for 25 to 30 minutes or until cake is golden brown and begins to pull away from sides of pan; cake is done when wooden pick inserted in center comes out clean. Invert pan on a wire rack and let cool completely; then remove from pan.

Split cake horizontally into 2 layers; place each layer on a platter. Drizzle 1 cup sherry over each layer; cover loosely with waxed paper or plastic wrap and let sit for 1 day.

Next day, spread 1 layer of cake with ½ cup apple jelly and sprinkle with ½ cup almonds; top with a layer of custard. Place remaining layer of cake on top, and repeat layers of jelly, almonds, and custard. Cover cake with plastic wrap and refrigerate 1 more day.

When ready to serve, frost cake with whipped cream frosting, and sprinkle with remaining ¼ cup almonds. If desired, serve with any remaining custard and whipped cream. Cake will keep up to 1 week when stored in refrigerator. Yield: one 10-inch cake.

Note: Tipsy Cake is best when prepared two or three days ahead to give the sherry time to season the cake.

Custard:

1½ cups sugar
¼ cup all-purpose flour
⅛ teaspoon salt
6 eggs, beaten
1 quart milk, scalded
2 teaspoons vanilla extract

Combine sugar, flour, and salt in top of double boiler; add eggs and beat well. Gradually add milk, stirring constantly until well blended. Cook over boiling water, stirring constantly, until mixture thickens and coats spoon.

Remove from heat and cool; stir in vanilla. If custard is not smooth, strain through a sieve or process in blender. Chill thoroughly. Yield: about 6 cups.

Whipped Cream Frosting:

2 cups whipping cream
3 tablespoons sugar
2 teaspoons vanilla extract

Whip cream until it begins to thicken. Gradually add sugar and vanilla, and continue beating until stiff peaks form. Yield: about 4 cups.

Tipsy Cake is an adaption of English trifle, a sherry-soaked cake served with preserves, custard, and whipped cream. Also known as Tipsy Squire and Tipsy Parson, it was originally served as a special dessert when the parson came to dine.

Confections

BOURBON PRALINES

    2 cups sugar
    1 teaspoon soda
    1 cup buttermilk
      Pinch of salt
    2 tablespoons butter or margarine
 2⅓ cups broken pecans or walnuts
    5 tablespoons bourbon

Combine sugar, soda, buttermilk, and salt in a large saucepan. Cook, stirring frequently, until candy thermometer registers 210°. Add butter and pecans. Cook, stirring constantly, to 230°.

Remove from heat, and stir in bourbon; cool about 1 minute. Beat by hand until mixture begins to thicken (about 5 minutes). Drop by tablespoonfuls onto waxed paper; let stand until firm. Yield: about 2½ dozen.

Mrs. J. John Stearman,
Louisville, Kentucky.

PECAN SNACKS

    1 tablespoon corn oil
    2 cups pecan halves
  ½ teaspoon onion powder
  ½ teaspoon garlic salt

Heat corn oil in a heavy skillet over moderate heat. Add pecans, onion powder, and garlic salt; stir constantly 1 minute. Remove from heat, and drain on paper towels. Yield: 2 cups.

Mrs. E. T. Williams,
Baton Rouge, Louisiana.

BUTTERMILK PECAN PRALINES

    2 cups sugar
    1 teaspoon soda
    1 cup buttermilk
    2 tablespoons butter or margarine
 2½ cups broken pecans
    1 teaspoon vanilla extract
      About 24 pecan halves

Combine sugar, soda, buttermilk, and butter in a large, heavy Dutch oven; cook over high heat 5 minutes, stirring constantly. Add broken pecans; cook, stirring constantly, over medium heat until candy thermometer registers 230°. Remove from heat; stir in vanilla. Beat just until mixture begins to thicken.

Working rapidly, drop mixture by tablespoonfuls onto lightly buttered waxed paper. Place a pecan half on each praline; cool. Store in an airtight container. Yield: about 2 dozen.

Mrs. Harold D. Lenard,
Columbia, Louisiana.

MILLIONAIRES

    1 (14-ounce) package caramels
    3 to 4 tablespoons milk
    2 cups pecan pieces
      Butter or margarine
    1 tablespoon shortening
    1 (12-ounce) package semisweet
      chocolate morsels

Melt caramels in milk over low heat; stir in pecans. Drop by teaspoonfuls onto buttered waxed paper. Chill. Melt shortening and chocolate morsels in a heavy saucepan over low heat; remove from heat. Dip candy into chocolate, and return to waxed paper. Chill. Yield: 3½ dozen.

Mrs. Jesse Bearden, Jr.,
Pine Bluff, Arkansas.

SWEDISH NUTS

1 cup whole almonds
½ cup butter or margarine
2 egg whites
1 cup sugar
 Dash of salt
1 cup walnut halves
1 cup pecan halves

Spread almonds on a cookie sheet. Roast at 325° until lightly browned, about 15 to 20 minutes, stirring occasionally; cool. Melt butter in oven in a 13- × 9- × 2-inch baking pan.

Beat egg whites until foamy; add sugar and salt, and continue beating until stiff. Fold in almonds, walnuts, and pecans; spread nut mixture in baking pan over melted butter.

Bake at 325° about 30 minutes or until mixture is browned and all butter is absorbed, stirring and turning every 10 minutes to cook evenly. Yield: about 4 cups.   *Mrs. Robert A. Wolfe,*
Doraville, Georgia.

GERMAN CHOCOLATE FUDGE

1 (12-ounce) package semisweet
 chocolate morsels
3 (4-ounce) bars sweet chocolate,
 broken into pieces
1 (7-ounce) jar marshmallow cream
4½ cups sugar
2 tablespoons butter or margarine
1 (13-ounce) can evaporated milk,
 undiluted
 Pinch of salt
2 cups chopped pecans or walnuts

Combine chocolate morsels, sweet chocolate, and marshmallow cream in a large bowl; set aside. Combine sugar, butter, milk, and salt in a heavy skillet. Bring mixture to a boil; boil 6 minutes, stirring constantly.

Pour hot syrup over chocolate mixture; stir with a wooden spoon until smooth. Add pecans,

and mix well. Spread fudge in a buttered jellyroll pan; when cool, cut into squares. Yield: about 5 pounds.   *Mrs. Berlin L. Hamilton,*
Newport News, Virginia.

CANDIED FRESH COCONUT

1 cup sugar
½ cup water
1 fresh coconut, sliced into ¼-inch
 strips

Combine sugar and water in a saucepan; cook, stirring constantly, until mixture spins a thread (230° on candy thermometer). Stir in coconut, and cook until syrup begins to sugar. Turn out on waxed paper, and separate strips. Yield: about 3 cups.   *Mrs. William C. Arnold,*
Marietta, Georgia.

CREAM CHEESE MINTS

2½ cups powdered sugar
1 (3-ounce) package cream cheese,
 softened
½ teaspoon peppermint extract
7 drops red food coloring
7 drops green food coloring
 Sugar

Cream powdered sugar and cream cheese together in a small bowl. Blend in peppermint extract. Divide mixture in half; add red food coloring to half of mixture and green food coloring to the other half. Knead until consistency of pie dough. Form dough into ½-inch balls; roll balls in sugar. Press into candy molds, and remove immediately. Yield: about 2 dozen mints.
Mrs. Jim Mack,
Midland, Texas.

Welcome the season's guests with our festive Holiday Log Cake and Strawberry Candies. Both are such attractive table decorations that you'll want to give them as holiday hostess gifts.

STRAWBERRY CANDIES

　1　(15-ounce) can sweetened condensed
　　　milk
　1　pound flaked coconut, finely ground
　2　(3-ounce) packages strawberry-
　　　flavored gelatin, divided
　1　cup finely ground almonds
　1　tablespoon sugar
　1　teaspoon vanilla extract
　1　(4½-ounce) can green decorator icing

Combine milk, coconut, 1 package gelatin, almonds, sugar, and vanilla; mix well. Shape mixture into strawberries. Roll candies in remaining gelatin, coating thoroughly. Let candies dry until firm. Make leaves with icing on top of candies. Store in a covered container. Yield: about 4 dozen. *Florence L. Costello,*
Chattanooga, Tennessee.

CANDIED CITRUS PEEL

　1　thick-skinned grapefruit
　2　thick-skinned oranges
　1　thick-skinned lemon
　1½　cups sugar
　　　Additional sugar
　　　Food coloring (optional)

Peel fruits. Cut peel into ¼- × 2-inch strips. Cover with cold water in a saucepan, and let come to a boil. Drain and repeat three times. Drain; add 1½ cups sugar. Cook over low heat, stirring until sugar dissolves. Continue to cook until peel becomes transparent and has absorbed all the syrup.

　Combine additional sugar and food coloring. Roll each piece in sugar. Store in covered container. Yield: 1 to 1½ cups.

Mrs. W. H. Smith,
Birmingham, Alabama.

Cookies

FROSTED APRICOT JEWELS

1¼ cups all-purpose flour
¼ cup sugar
1½ teaspoons baking powder
¼ teaspoon salt
½ cup butter or margarine, softened
1 (3-ounce) package cream cheese, softened
½ cup flaked coconut
½ cup apricot preserves
   Frosting (recipe follows)
   Pecan halves

Combine flour, sugar, baking powder, and salt; cut in butter and cream cheese until mixture resembles coarse meal. Add coconut and preserves, mixing well.

Drop dough by teaspoonfuls onto ungreased cookie sheets. Bake at 350° for 15 to 18 minutes or until lightly browned. Cool completely on a wire rack. Spread each cookie with frosting, and top with a pecan half. Yield: about 3 dozen.

Frosting:

1 cup sifted powdered sugar
1 tablespoon butter or margarine, softened
¼ cup apricot preserves

Combine all ingredients, and beat until smooth. Yield: 1 cup.   *Mrs. Mike Raybon, Duncanville, Texas.*

COCONUT ISLAND COOKIES

3 (1-ounce) squares unsweetened chocolate
¼ cup strong coffee
½ cup shortening
1 cup firmly packed brown sugar
1 egg
2 cups all-purpose flour
½ teaspoon salt
½ teaspoon soda
⅔ cup commercial sour cream
1 cup flaked coconut, divided
   Chocolate frosting (recipe follows)

Combine chocolate and coffee in a small saucepan; place over low heat, stirring until chocolate melts. Set aside to cool.

Combine shortening and brown sugar, creaming until light and fluffy; beat in egg and chocolate mixture. Combine flour, salt, and soda; add to creamed mixture alternately with sour cream, mixing well after each addition. Stir in ⅓ cup coconut.

Drop dough by teaspoonfuls onto greased baking sheets. Bake at 375° for 12 to 15 minutes. Frost with chocolate frosting while warm, and sprinkle with remaining coconut. Let stand on wire racks until frosting sets. Yield: about 6 dozen.

Chocolate Frosting:

1½ (1-ounce) squares unsweetened chocolate
¼ cup commercial sour cream
1 tablespoon butter or margarine
1 to 1½ cups sifted powdered sugar

Combine chocolate, sour cream, and butter in a small heavy saucepan; place over low heat, stirring until chocolate is melted. Remove from heat, and stir in enough powdered sugar to make frosting a spreading consistency. If necessary, reheat occasionally to maintain consistency. Yield: 1¼ cups.

Mrs. Charles R. Field, Bryson City, North Carolina.

FRUITCAKE COOKIES

½ cup butter or margarine, softened
½ cup firmly packed light brown sugar
2 eggs, beaten
¼ cup buttermilk
1½ cups self-rising flour
½ teaspoon soda
½ teaspoon ground allspice
½ teaspoon ground cinnamon
1 cup chopped candied cherries
1 cup chopped candied pineapple
1 cup chopped dates
1½ cups raisins (optional)
3 cups pecans, chopped

Combine butter and sugar, creaming until light and fluffy. Add eggs, buttermilk, flour, soda, and spices; mix well. Stir in remaining ingredients. Drop by teaspoonfuls onto greased baking sheets. Bake at 300° for 25 minutes. Yield: about 7 dozen.

Mary Ann Ferguson,
Union City, Tennessee.

DATE-NUT PINWHEEL COOKIES

1 (8-ounce) package dates, chopped
1 cup sugar
1 cup hot water
1 cup very finely chopped walnuts
2 cups firmly packed brown sugar
1 cup butter or margarine, softened
2 eggs
3½ cups all-purpose flour
½ teaspoon soda
½ teaspoon cream of tartar
½ teaspoon salt
1 teaspoon vanilla extract

Combine dates, sugar, and hot water in a medium saucepan; cook over medium heat until thickened (about 6 to 8 minutes), stirring constantly. Remove from heat, and stir in walnuts; set aside to cool.

Combine brown sugar and butter, creaming until light and fluffy; beat in eggs. Combine flour, soda, cream of tartar, and salt; stir into creamed mixture. Add vanilla, and mix well.

Divide dough into thirds. Roll each portion into a 12-inch square on waxed paper; spread with one-third of date mixture. Lifting up edge of waxed paper, gently peel off dough and roll jellyroll fashion. Wrap rolls in waxed paper, and chill overnight.

Cut dough into ¼-inch slices, and place 2 inches apart on greased cookie sheets. Bake at 350° for 8 to 10 minutes. Cool cookies on wire racks. Yield: about 6 dozen.

Mrs. Fred McLeod,
Valdosta, Georgia.

CHERRY DELIGHTS

1 cup butter or margarine, softened
½ cup sugar
½ cup light corn syrup
2 eggs, separated
2½ cups all-purpose flour
2 cups finely chopped pecans
Candied cherry halves

Combine butter and sugar, creaming until light and fluffy. Add corn syrup, egg yolks, and flour; mix well. Chill.

Lightly beat egg whites. Shape dough into 1-inch balls; dip each in egg whites, and coat with pecans. Press a cherry half, cut side down, into center of each.

Place cookies about 1½ inches apart on greased baking sheets. Bake at 325° for 20 minutes. Yield: 4 dozen.

Mrs. Arlano Funderburk,
Levelland, Texas.

Special cookies are as much a part of the holidays as hanging the Christmas stocking: (clockwise from top left) Coconut Island Cookies, Date-Nut Pinwheel Cookies, Cherry Delights, Frosted Apricot Jewels, Fruitcake Cookies, Date-Nut Balls, Lemon Cheese Logs, Candy Cane Cookies, Cream Cheese Crescents, Black-Eyed Susans, and Old-Fashioned Christmas Cookies.

CANDY CANE COOKIES

- ½ cup shortening
- ½ cup butter or margarine, softened
- 1 cup powdered sugar
- 1 egg, slightly beaten
- 1 teaspoon almond extract
- 1 teaspoon vanilla extract
- 2½ cups all-purpose flour
- 1 teaspoon salt
- ½ teaspoon red food coloring
- ⅓ cup finely crushed peppermint candy
- ⅓ cup sugar

Cream shortening and butter in a large mixing bowl until fluffy; add next 6 ingredients and mix well. Divide dough in half; add food coloring to one portion, mixing well.

On a lightly floured surface, roll a teaspoonful of each dough (plain and colored) into a 4½-inch-long rope. Place ropes side by side, and carefully twist together; curve one end down to resemble a cane. Repeat procedure with remaining dough.

Place cookies on ungreased cookie sheets, and bake at 375° for 9 minutes or just until edges begin to brown. Combine candy and sugar, mixing well. Remove cookies from cookie sheet while warm; immediately coat with candy mixture. Yield: about 4 dozen.

Mrs. H. S. Wright,
Charlotte, North Carolina.

FILLED CHRISTMAS COOKIES

½ cup shortening
1 cup sugar
1 egg, beaten
½ cup milk
1 teaspoon vanilla extract
3½ cups all-purpose flour
1 teaspoon soda
2 teaspoons cream of tartar
  Preserves

Cream shortening and sugar until light and fluffy; stir in egg. Combine milk and vanilla; set aside. Combine flour, soda, and cream of tartar; add to creamed mixture alternately with milk mixture, beginning and ending with flour mixture and mixing well after each addition.

Roll half of dough on lightly floured board to ⅛-inch thickness; cut with 2-inch round cookie cutters. Place on lightly greased baking sheets; spread 1 teaspoon preserves over each.

Roll remaining dough to ⅛-inch thickness; cut with 2-inch round cookie cutters. Cut a 1-inch round center from each cookie round; place doughnut-shaped round over cookie rounds spread with preserves. Lightly press outer edges together.

Bake at 350° for 10 minutes or until lightly browned. Yield: about 4 dozen.

Mary L. Butler,
Decaturville, Tennessee.

CREAM CHEESE CRESCENTS

1 cup butter or margarine, softened
1 (8-ounce) package cream cheese, softened
2 cups all-purpose flour
¼ teaspoon salt
¾ cup finely chopped walnuts
⅓ cup sugar
1½ teaspoons ground cinnamon
  Powdered sugar

Combine butter and cream cheese, creaming until well blended. Combine flour and salt; add to creamed mixture, mixing well. Shape dough into 8 balls; wrap each in plastic wrap, and chill at least 2 hours.

Roll each ball of dough into an 8-inch circle on a lightly floured surface; cut into 8 wedges. Combine walnuts, sugar, and cinnamon; sprinkle ¼ teaspoon mixture over each wedge of dough. Starting at wide edge of dough, roll up each wedge; shape into a crescent. Place point side down on ungreased cookie sheets.

Bake crescents at 350° for 12 minutes or until lightly browned. Cool and dust with powdered sugar. Yield: about 5 dozen.

Bobby Carnes,
Interlachen, Florida.

LEMON CHEESE LOGS

1 cup sugar
1 cup butter or margarine, softened
1 (3-ounce) package cream cheese, softened
1 egg yolk
2½ cups all-purpose flour
1 cup finely chopped walnuts
½ teaspoon salt
½ teaspoon grated lemon rind
1 (6-ounce) package semisweet chocolate morsels
  Decorator candies

Combine sugar, butter, and cream cheese; cream until light and fluffy. Add egg yolk, beating well. Stir in flour, walnuts, salt, and lemon rind; mix well. Cover and chill at least 2 hours.

Shape dough by tablespoons into 2-inch logs by rolling between palms of hands. Place cookies on ungreased baking sheets, and bake at 325° for 12 minutes or until lightly browned. Cool completely on wire racks.

Melt chocolate morsels in a small saucepan over low heat. Dip one end of each log in melted chocolate, and sprinkle with decorator candy. Let stand on wire racks until chocolate sets. Store between layers of waxed paper in an airtight container. Cookies may be frozen. Yield: 12 dozen.

Mrs. E. L. Cromer,
Anderson, South Carolina.

BLACK-EYED SUSANS

½ cup butter or margarine, softened
½ cup sugar
½ cup firmly packed brown sugar
1 egg
1½ tablespoons warm water
1 teaspoon vanilla extract
1 cup peanut butter
1½ cups all-purpose flour
½ teaspoon salt
½ teaspoon soda
About ½ cup semisweet chocolate morsels

Combine butter and sugar, creaming until light and fluffy; add egg, warm water, vanilla, and peanut butter; beat mixture well.

Combine dry ingredients; add to creamed mixture, mixing well. Using a cookie press with a flower-shaped disc, press dough onto lightly greased cookie sheets. Place a chocolate morsel in the center of each flower.

Bake at 350° for 8 minutes or until lightly browned. Remove to wire racks, and cool completely. Chill 30 minutes to firm up chocolate centers. Yield: about 10 dozen 1-inch cookies.

Noella C. Peterson,
Knoxville, Tennessee.

DATE-NUT BALLS

½ cup butter or margarine
¾ cup sugar
1 (8-ounce) package dates, chopped
2½ cups crisp rice cereal
1 cup chopped pecans
Flaked coconut or powdered sugar

Combine butter, sugar, and dates in a medium saucepan. Bring to a boil; cook, stirring constantly, for 3 minutes. Stir in cereal and pecans; cool to touch. Shape into 1-inch balls, and roll each in coconut. Yield: about 4 dozen.

Emily Baker,
Montgomery, Alabama.

OLD-FASHIONED CHRISTMAS COOKIES

1 cup butter or margarine, softened
2 cups sugar
¼ cup firmly packed brown sugar
2 eggs
¼ cup plus 2 tablespoons milk
2 teaspoons vanilla extract
4 cups all-purpose flour
2 teaspoons baking powder
½ teaspoon salt
Decorator candies
Decorator icing

Cream butter and sugar until light and fluffy; add eggs, mixing well. Stir in milk and vanilla. Combine flour, baking powder, and salt; add to creamed mixture, mixing well. Chill.

Roll dough out on a lightly floured board to ⅛-inch thickness; cut with shaped cookie cutters. Place on lightly greased baking sheets; bake at 350° for 10 to 12 minutes.

Decorate as desired with decorator candies and icing. Yield: about 5 dozen.

Sandy Dyer,
Roanoke, Virginia.

GINGERBREAD FAMILY COOKIES

1¾ cups sugar
¾ cup honey
¼ cup butter or margarine
⅓ cup lemon juice
 1 tablespoon finely grated lemon rind
 6 cups all-purpose flour
¼ cup plus 2 tablespoons baking powder
⅛ teaspoon salt
1½ teaspoons ground ginger
 1 teaspoon ground cinnamon
¼ teaspoon ground nutmeg
¼ teaspoon ground cloves
 1 egg, well beaten
 1 egg yolk, well beaten
   Royal Icing
   Assorted candies and sprinkles

Note: Using the decorating diagrams (pages 90-91) as a guide to the general shape, cut two patterns, one 14 × 10½ inches for the grownups and one 9½ × 7¼ inches for the children.

Combine sugar, honey, and butter in a 4-quart heavy saucepan. Bring to a boil, stirring constantly until sugar dissolves. Remove from heat. Add lemon juice and lemon rind. Mix well. Cool to room temperature.

Combine flour, baking powder, salt, and spices; stir well. Add 2 cups flour mixture, egg, and egg yolk to liquid mixture; mix well. Gradually add remaining flour mixture; mix well (dough will be stiff). Shape into a ball with lightly floured hands. Lightly knead dough until smooth.

Place three-fourths of dough on a greased and floured 16- × 12-inch cookie sheet. Roll dough to 3/16 to 1/4-inch thickness, covering entire

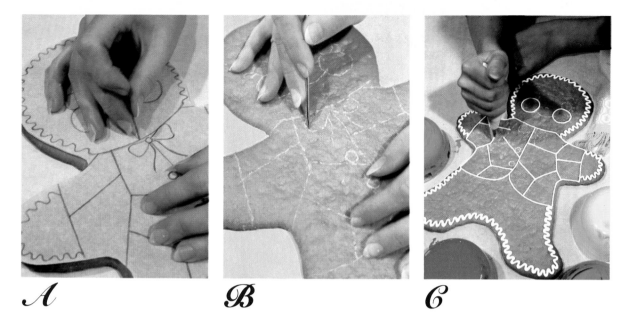

A   B   C

cookie sheet. Arrange patterns for 1 large or 2 small gingerbread figures on cookie sheet. Cut around pattern with the tip of a knife. Remove excess dough. Combine with remaining dough, wrap in waxed paper and refrigerate.

Bake cookies at 325° for 30 minutes or until firm and golden brown. Remove from oven. Carefully slip a spatula under cookies to loosen. Let cool for 1 minute on cookie sheet. Transfer to wire rack to complete cooling. Repeat procedure with remaining dough.

Decorate the cookies with Royal Icing, assorted candies, and decorator sprinkles according to instructions. Yield: 1 large and 2 small gingerbread cookies.

Royal Icing:

  3 **large egg whites**
  ½ **teaspoon cream of tartar**
  1 **(16-ounce) package powdered sugar,
     sifted**

Combine egg whites and cream of tartar in a large mixing bowl. Beat at medium speed of electric mixer until frothy. Gradually add powdered sugar and continue beating for 5 to 7 minutes. Yield: about 2 cups.

Note: Royal Icing dries very quickly; keep covered at all times with a damp towel. Do not double this recipe. If additional icing is needed, make two batches.

Draw face and clothes onto cookie patterns following diagram for clothing. Place pattern on cookie and using a large needle, punch holes through lines onto the cookie to mark placement of clothes. Lift pattern and connect dots on cookie by scratching lines onto cookie with a needle (Photos A and B).

Use parchment paper bag and metal decorating tip No. 3. Fill bag half full of Royal Icing. Pipe icing on top of lines for face and clothes. Pipe icing on cookie for head, hands, and feet in a rickrack design (Photo C).

Spoon a small amount of Royal Icing into separate bowls for each color desired, leaving a small amount of icing white. Set aside small amount of icing the color of which you desire to make bows on clothes; carefully add enough water to each remaining bowl of icing, a small amount at a time, to make mixture a flowing consistency. (Keep icing covered.)

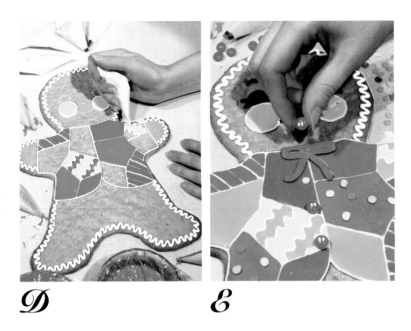

$\mathscr{D}$ $\mathscr{E}$

Fill parchment paper bags about half full of flow-in icing. Snip off small tip of cone and apply icing to cover areas between outline with desired color. Spread the icing into hard-to-reach areas using a toothpick (Photo D).

Work with one color at a time, allowing icing to dry before changing colors. Try to avoid using excess icing as it will spill over into another color area. If the flow-in icing is too watery, it will not dry properly and may run under outline into other color areas. If air bubbles form in icing, use a clean straight pin to remove them. Wipe pin clean between each use.

Make ribbon bows with regular consistency icing using tip No. 101.

Attach various cake decorations and candies after flow-in icing has begun to harden, using Royal Icing (Photo E).

Note: Store cookies in airtight container at room temperature or in freezer. Avoid making during humid weather because icing will not dry properly, and cookies tend to pick up moisture and become soft.

Jams, Jellies & Relishes

BRANDIED PEAR SAUCE

5 ripe pears, peeled, cored, and
   quartered
1 orange, peeled and sliced
1 cup sugar
1 teaspoon ground cloves
½ cup fruit-flavored brandy (apricot,
   cherry, orange, etc.)

Combine fruit and sugar in a Dutch oven, mixing well. Cover and cook until fruit is very soft (about 30 minutes). Process fruit mixture in electric blender until smooth, or put through food grinder or sieve.

Pour fruit mixture back into Dutch oven, and add cloves and brandy; cook until mixture is as thick as applesauce (about 1 hour). Pour into hot, sterilized jars. Cover at once with metal lids, and screw metal bands tight. Process in boiling-water bath 20 minutes. Yield: about 2 pints.

Ruth Weddle,
Tulsa, Oklahoma.

PEAR PRESERVES

3 quarts peeled and diced pears
3 cups water
4½ cups sugar
6 lemon slices (optional)

If pears are firm, cook in boiling water until almost tender; drain. Combine 3 cups water and sugar and bring to a boil; add pears to syrup and bring to a boil. Add lemon slices, if desired. Boil rapidly until pears are clear and tender. Pour fruit into hot sterilized jars, leaving ⅛-inch headspace. Cover at once with metal lids, and screw metal bands tight. Process in boiling-water bath 10 minutes. Yield: about 4 pints.

PEACH-PECAN JAM

6 cups sliced fresh peaches
6 cups sugar
⅔ cup chopped pecans or walnuts

Combine peaches and sugar in a heavy saucepan; stir well. Bring to a boil. Reduce heat; simmer until thick (about 30 minutes), stirring occasionally. Remove from heat; stir in pecans. Spoon into hot sterilized jelly jars. Cover at once with metal lids and screw metal bands tight. Process in boiling-water bath for 10 minutes. Yield: 6 half pints.

Note: Jam may be served over ice cream. Chill 8 hours before using as a topping.

Mrs. Charles Kelly,
Atlanta, Georgia

CRANBERRY JELLY

1 quart cranberry juice cocktail
¼ cup plus 2 tablespoons powdered fruit
  pectin
4 cups sugar
¼ cup lemon juice

Combine cranberry juice cocktail and pectin in a large saucepan; stir over high heat until mixture comes to full boil. Stir in sugar, and return to a full boil; boil hard 2 minutes, stirring constantly. Remove from heat, and stir in lemon juice.

Skim off foam with a metal spoon, and pour quickly into sterilized jelly glasses, leaving ½-inch headspace. Seal at once with ⅛-inch layer of hot paraffin. Yield: about 7 pints.

Mrs. Art Cook,
Lubbock, Texas.

CRANBERRY CHUTNEY

4 cups fresh cranberries
2 cups sugar
1 cup water
1 cup orange juice
1 cup raisins
1 cup chopped walnuts
1 cup chopped celery
1 cup chopped apple
1 tablespoon grated orange rind
1 teaspoon ground ginger

Combine cranberries, sugar, and water; cook over low heat 15 minutes, stirring frequently. Remove from heat; stir in remaining ingredients. Cover and refrigerate. Yield: 7 cups.

Hazel Stove,
Ooltewah, Tennessee.

PEPPER JELLY

¾ cup ground green pepper
¼ cup ground hot pepper
6 cups sugar
1½ cups vinegar
2 (3-ounce) packages liquid fruit pectin

Combine pepper, sugar, and vinegar in a large saucepan. Place over high heat, and stir until mixture comes to a hard boil. Boil hard 1 minute, stirring constantly.

Remove from heat; stir in pectin. Let sit 5 minutes. Skim off foam with a metal spoon, and pour quickly into hot sterilized jelly glasses, leaving ½-inch headspace. Seal at once with ⅛-inch layer of hot paraffin or metal lids. Yield: 6 cups.

Pies

CORN RELISH

- ½ cup sugar
- ½ teaspoon salt
- ½ teaspoon celery seeds
- ¼ teaspoon dry mustard
- ⅛ teaspoon white pepper
- ½ cup cider vinegar
- 1 (17-ounce) can whole kernel corn, drained
- 2 tablespoons diced green pepper
- 1 (4-ounce) jar pimiento, diced
- 1 tablespoon instant minced onion

Combine sugar, salt, celery seeds, mustard, pepper, and vinegar in a 1-quart saucepan; bring to a boil. Boil 2 minutes, and remove from heat. Stir in corn, green pepper, pimiento, and onion. Cool. Pour into a pint jar. Cover tightly, and refrigerate several days before serving. Yield: 1 pint.
Mrs. W. K. Williams,
Huntington, West Virginia.

HOLIDAY RELISH

- 1 pound whole raw cranberries, ground
- 2 apples, washed, cored, and finely chopped
  Juice of 2 oranges
- 1 (8-ounce) can crushed pineapple
- 1 cup chopped pecans
- 2¾ cups sugar

Combine all ingredients, mixing well. Cover and refrigerate overnight. Yield: about 2 quarts.
Elizabeth Kraus,
Louisville, Kentucky.

ORANGE-COCONUT PIE

- 1 cup sugar
- 3 tablespoons cornstarch
- 3 tablespoons all-purpose flour
- ¼ teaspoon salt
- 1½ cups water
- ¾ cup orange juice
- 1 tablespoon lemon juice
- 3 egg yolks, lightly beaten
- ¾ cup flaked coconut, divided
  Grated rind of 1 orange
- 1 baked 9-inch pastry shell
- 3 egg whites
- 6 tablespoons sugar

Combine 1 cup sugar, cornstarch, flour, and salt in a heavy saucepan; stir in water, orange juice, and lemon juice. Cook over low heat until thickened, stirring constantly.

Gradually stir about one-fourth of hot mixture into egg yolks; add to remaining hot mixture, stirring constantly. Cook 2 minutes longer, stirring constantly. Remove from heat, and stir in ½ cup coconut and orange rind. Pour filling into pastry shell.

Beat egg whites (at room temperature) until foamy. Gradually add 6 tablespoons sugar, 1 tablespoon at a time, beating until stiff peaks form. Spread meringue over filling, and seal edges well.

Bake pie at 350° for 15 minutes. Sprinkle with remaining coconut, and bake 2 minutes longer. Cool. Yield: one 9-inch pie.
Dora Farrar,
Gadsden, Alabama.

MINCEMEAT CRUNCH PIE

1 (28-ounce) jar prepared mincemeat
1 unbaked 9-inch pastry shell
1 tablespoon instant orange peel
¼ cup all-purpose flour
¼ cup firmly packed brown sugar
2 tablespoons margarine, softened
¼ cup chopped pecans or walnuts

Spoon mincemeat into pastry shell; sprinkle with orange peel.

Combine flour and sugar in a bowl. Using a pastry blender or two knives, cut in margarine until mixture resembles coarse meal. Stir in pecans. Sprinkle mixture over pie. Bake at 425° for 25 to 30 minutes. Yield: one 9-inch pie.

Mrs. Thomas Lee Adams,
Kingsport, Tennessee.

GRASSHOPPER PIE

1¼ cups chocolate wafer crumbs
⅓ cup butter or margarine, melted
⅔ cup milk
24 large marshmallows
¼ cup green crème de menthe
2 tablespoons white crème de cacao
1 cup whipping cream, whipped
Chocolate wafer crumbs (optional)

Combine 1¼ cups crumbs and butter; press into an 8-inch piepan, and chill well.

Combine milk and marshmallows in a heavy saucepan; cook over low heat, stirring often, until marshmallows melt. Cool to room temperature. Fold liqueurs and whipped cream into marshmallow mixture. Spoon into pie shell; garnish with chocolate wafer crumbs, if desired. Freeze 4 to 6 hours. Yield: one 8-inch pie.

Margaret Staszak,
De Soto, Texas.

FAVORITE PECAN PIE

1 unbaked 9-inch pastry shell
3 eggs
1 cup sugar
1 cup light corn syrup
2 tablespoons butter or margarine, melted
⅛ teaspoon salt
1 teaspoon vanilla extract
About 1½ cups pecan halves

Prick bottom and sides of pastry shell; bake at 400° for 5 minutes. Set aside to cool.

Beat eggs until light and lemon colored; add sugar and corn syrup, beating until fluffy. Stir in butter, salt, and vanilla.

Pour filling into pastry shell. Top with pecan halves.

Bake at 300° for 1 hour and 45 minutes or until center of pie is firm. Yield: one 9-inch pie.

Claudia Galvan,
Dallas, Texas.

CRANBERRY MERINGUE PIE

2 cups sugar
1 cup water
4 cups fresh cranberries
4 eggs, separated
2½ tablespoons all-purpose flour
Dash of salt
3 tablespoons butter or margarine
½ teaspoon almond extract
1 baked 9-inch pastry shell
¼ cup powdered sugar

Combine sugar and water in a saucepan; bring to a boil. Add cranberries; cook about 10 minutes or until the skins pop.

Beat egg yolks; stir in flour and salt. Gradually stir about one-fourth of hot cranberry mixture into yolk mixture; add to remaining hot mixture, stirring constantly. Cook over low heat, stirring constantly, about 5 minutes or until mixture thickens. Remove from heat; stir in butter and almond extract. Let mixture cool. Pour into baked pastry shell.

Beat egg whites (at room temperature) until foamy. Gradually add powdered sugar, beating until stiff peaks form. Spread meringue over pie, sealing to edge of pastry. Bake at 300° about 25 minutes or until meringue is browned. Cool thoroughly before serving. Yield: one 9-inch pie.

Ruth Hormanskie,
Melbourne Beach, Florida.

CHOCOLATE-EGGNOG LAYER PIE

    1 envelope unflavored gelatin
    ½ cup cold water
    ⅓ cup sugar
    2 tablespoons cornstarch
    ¼ teaspoon salt
    2 cups commercial eggnog
    1½ squares unsweetened chocolate,
        melted
    1 teaspoon vanilla extract
    1 baked 9-inch pastry shell
    1 teaspoon rum extract
    2 cups whipping cream, divided
    ¼ cup powdered sugar
      Chocolate curls (optional)

Soften gelatin in cold water; set aside. Combine sugar, cornstarch, and salt in a 1-quart saucepan; gradually stir in eggnog. Cook over medium heat, stirring constantly, until thickened; cook 2 minutes. Remove from heat, and add gelatin mixture; stir until dissolved.

Divide filling in half; set one half aside to cool. Add melted chocolate and vanilla to other half of filling; stir well and pour into pastry shell. Chill until filling is set.

Add rum extract to remaining filling. Beat 1 cup whipping cream until soft peaks form, and fold into filling mixture. Spoon over chocolate layer and chill.

Beat remaining whipping cream until foamy; gradually add powdered sugar, beating until soft peaks form. Spread over pie; garnish with chocolate curls, if desired. Yield: one 9-inch pie.

Mrs. Robert Pender,
Port Tobacco, Maryland.

BOURBON PIE

    1 envelope unflavored gelatin
    ½ cup cold water
    1½ cups milk
    ¾ cup sugar
    3 tablespoons cornstarch
    3 eggs, well beaten
    1 tablespoon butter
    ¼ cup bourbon
    ½ teaspoon vanilla extract
    1 cup whipping cream, whipped
    1 baked 10-inch pastry shell
      Ground nutmeg

Soften gelatin in cold water; set aside.

Scald milk in top of double boiler; combine sugar and cornstarch, and add to milk. Cook, stirring constantly, until thick. Cook an additional 15 minutes, stirring often.

Gradually stir about one-fourth of hot mixture into eggs; add to remaining hot mixture, and cook 1 minute longer. Stir in butter and gelatin. Chill 30 minutes in refrigerator, but do not let mixture gel.

Add bourbon and vanilla; blend well. Fold in whipped cream; pour into pastry shell. Sprinkle with nutmeg. Chill 4 to 6 hours before serving. Yield: one 10-inch pie.   *Margaret K. Johnson,*
Kansas City, Missouri.

Specialties

CHARLOTTE RUSSE

  4 eggs, separated
 10 tablespoons sugar, divided
  1 envelope unflavored gelatin
 ½ cup cold water
  2 cups whipping cream, whipped
  1 teaspoon vanilla extract
 12 to 18 ladyfingers

Beat egg yolks and 4 tablespoons sugar until thick and lemon colored; set aside. Soften gelatin in cold water; place over hot water and stir until dissolved. Add gelatin to yolk mixture.

Beat egg whites in a large bowl; gradually add 6 tablespoons sugar and continue to beat until stiff peaks form. Reserve ½ cup whipped cream for garnish. Fold remaining whipped cream, yolk mixture, and vanilla into egg whites.

Split ladyfingers in half lengthwise. Line an 8-cup glass or crystal bowl with ladyfingers. Pour in filling; chill until set. Garnish with reserved ½ cup whipped cream. Yield: 8 to 10 servings.

Note: Individual compotes may be used. Quarter ladyfingers lengthwise. Line compotes, and fill as directed.   *Mrs. Karl Koenig,*
Dallas, Texas.

Though this elegant dessert originated in Europe, it is very popular at Christmastime throughout the South. It consists of a molded shell of ladyfingers filled with a luscious Bavarian cream.

AMBROSIA

  6 oranges, peeled and sectioned
 ½ cup sugar or to taste
  1 coconut, grated

Place a layer of orange sections in a glass bowl; sprinkle with sugar, and layer with coconut. Repeat layers, ending with coconut. Chill. Yield: about 6 servings.   *Mrs. Robert Bruce,*
College Park, Maryland.

ORANGE BUTTER

  8 oranges, quartered and seeded
  5 pounds sugar (about 10 cups)
  1 (20-ounce) can crushed pineapple, undrained
 ½ cup butter or margarine

Grind orange quarters in food grinder, food processor, or electric blender; then combine all ingredients in a Dutch oven. Cook, stirring constantly, until mixture is thick (about 40 minutes).

Pour into sterilized jars; adjust lids, and process in boiling-water bath 10 minutes. Yield: about 5 pints.   *Mrs. David Ehmig,*
Sanford, North Carolina.

TOASTED PECANS

 ½ cup butter or margarine, melted
  3 cups pecan halves
     Salt to taste

Pour butter over pecans, stirring to coat well. Arrange pecans in a single layer on a baking sheet; sprinkle with salt. Bake at 275° about 1 hour; stir occasionally. Yield: 3 cups.
Mrs. Claude Workman, Jr.,
Memphis, Tennessee.

Traditional desserts enrich Christmas: (clockwise from top) Holiday Coconut Cake, Tipsy Cake, Charlotte Russe, Ambrosia, and Kentucky Bourbon Cake.

BARBECUED PECANS

2 tablespoons butter or margarine,
  melted
¼ cup Worcestershire sauce
1 tablespoon catsup
⅛ teaspoon hot sauce
4 cups pecan halves
  Salt (optional)

Combine first 4 ingredients; stir in pecans, and mix well. Spread pecans evenly in a shallow baking pan. Bake at 300° for 30 minutes, stirring frequently. Drain on paper towels. Sprinkle with salt, if desired. Yield: 4 cups.   *Junetta Davis,*
Norman, Oklahoma.

CHEESE CROCK

4 cups (16 ounces), shredded sharp
  Cheddar cheese
1 (3-ounce) package cream cheese
2 tablespoons olive oil
1½ teaspoons dry mustard
1¼ teaspoons minced garlic
3 tablespoons brandy

Let cheeses stand at room temperature until soft; blend together until very smooth. Add olive oil, mustard, garlic, and brandy, blending well. Pack into a stoneware cheese crock; cover and refrigerate at least 1 week before serving. To serve, allow cheese to soften at room temperature 1 hour; serve on crackers, melba toast, or party rye bread. Yield: about 3 cups.

Note: Cheese can be kept going as long as part of the original mixture is left. To add to crock, any firm cheese such as Cheddar, Swiss, Jack, etc. may be used. Shred any cheese scraps and blend with a small amount of cream cheese and olive oil until smooth; add beer, sherry, kirsch, or brandy, keeping the original proportion the same. Let mixture age a few days before serving again.   *Mrs. J. Russell Buchanan,*
Prospect, Kentucky.

HOMEMADE GRANOLA

5 cups regular oats, uncooked
1 cup sunflower seeds
1 cup flaked coconut
1 cup chopped pecans
1 cup sesame seeds
1 cup soy flour
1 cup nonfat dry milk solids
1 cup wheat germ
1 cup honey
1 cup milk
1 cup vegetable oil

Combine first 8 ingredients, and mix well. Combine honey, milk, and oil; pour over dry mixture, and stir until well blended. Spread mixture on cookie sheets; bake at 300° for 1 hour, stirring often. Cool and store granola in an airtight container until serving time. Yield: about 3 quarts.
Jan Uecke,
Fort Bliss, Texas.

HOMEMADE CURRY POWDER

1 (1-inch-square) piece fresh ginger,
  peeled and chopped
30 dried red chili peppers
4 dried green chili peppers
10 cardamom pods
10 whole cloves
4 (2-inch) cinnamon sticks
4 bay leaves
2½ tablespoons dried mint
2 teaspoons whole peppercorns
2 teaspoons cumin seeds
2 teaspoons poppy seeds
2 teaspoons mustard seeds
2 teaspoons ground coriander
1 teaspoon ground turmeric

Combine all ingredients in container of electric blender; blend at high speed 20 to 30 seconds. Store in an airtight container. Yield: ¾ cup.
M. J. Burgess,
Fort Worth, Texas.

The Joys of Giving

Giving is the very essence of Christmas. Not only is it a time when we give presents to represent our love for people, but it is also a time when we give the most of ourselves—those precious gifts of time, of sharing, of patience, and of love. "The Joys of Giving" is a chapter designed to inspire your holiday gift-giving and to bring fresh ideas and enthusiasm to your Christmas shopping.

Handicrafts and Christmas are a natural combination. Perhaps because this is a time of the year when we enjoy making things ourselves, it is also a time when we particularly enjoy and appreciate the handiwork of talented craftsmen. To give a handmade gift seems to say that we still value things that are carefully, lovingly made, and that we value the recipient enough to select just such a special gift. Over 30 one-of-a-kind "Handcrafted Treasures" are made available for you to order directly from The Southern Highland Handicraft Guild, an organization of talent that represents the best of our Southern heritage.

"Eleventh-Hour Gifts" offers a collection of gift suggestions for you to pull together at the last minute, because no matter how organized you may be during the holidays, there is sure to be the inevitable, unsolveable shopping puzzle as the 24th of December draws closer. Use these ideas as inspiration, adapting the contents of each surprise package to suit your own gift list.

"Holiday Delights" is an exceptional list of mail-order sources for foodstuffs for you to stock your own pantry or to send as gifts. Everything for holiday entertaining is included from exotic smoked salmon and caviar to aged cheeses and fruit boxes to delectable milk chocolate Christmas cards complete with a message. Fresh greenery wreaths and garlands are not forgotten in this chapter that puts everything you need for a most joyous Christmas just a mail order away.

Handcrafted Treasures

Over 30 original handcrafted gifts are featured in this section, each made by expert southern craftsmen who are members of The Southern Highland Handicraft Guild. The Guild was established in 1930 as a non-profit organization to further the talents of local craftsmen and the collective traditions of the Southern Appalachian Mountains and to provide marketing channels for the crafts. The high levels of craftsmanship and the design abilities of its over 600 members have earned for the Guild a valued and respected reputation among Southerners.

To enjoy a broad selection of imaginative craft ideas, illustrated by the carefully chosen items on the following pages, attend one of the Guild fairs, held in the Asheville, North Carolina, civic center. (Before travelling long distances, check with the Guild regarding changes in fair dates.)

October Fair 1981—October 15-17
July Fair 1982—July 22-25

All of the craft objects are guaranteed to be of high quality. Since individuality is the nature of a handmade craft, however, you should expect slight variations in coloration and pattern from that pictured. Crafts that do not meet your expectations may be returned within 30 days for a full refund. The following terms apply to all of the crafts ordered from this section through Crafts of Nine States, Inc., the marketing subsidiary of The Southern Highland Handicraft Guild.

SHIPPING: Craft items will be shipped United Parcel Service, so please include your street address and house or apartment number with each order. (Addresses with post office box numbers will be shipped Parcel Post.) Only those orders received by December 8, 1981, can be guaranteed for Christmas delivery.

POSTAGE, HANDLING & INSURANCE: Charges are given in parentheses after the price.

PRICE: The price of each craft item is guaranteed through January 15, 1982; after January 15, the items may still be available, but you should contact the Guild to verify prices before ordering.

TO ORDER: Please describe each item clearly, make checks or money orders payable to Crafts of Nine States, Inc. (North Carolina residents add 4% sales tax), and send, along with your street mailing address, to:

Crafts of Nine States, Inc.
Department OB/CC
P.O. Box 9545
Asheville, North Carolina 28815

Since these gifts are all made by hand, quantities are limited. Order early to avoid disappointment.

જ્જ

WINDCHIMES by Richard Davidson
of Asheville, North Carolina
Made of brass, bronze, copper, and stainless steel; will not rust, tangle, or break.
Penny windchime, 21″ × 2″ assembled.
$11.50 (1.70)
All-metal windchime, 25″ × 6″ assembled.
$22.50 (2.00)

HANGING PLANTER by Morgan Davies
of Leicester, North Carolina
Made of stoneware clay with black slip decoration, 7″ diameter, 9″ height.
$41.50 (4.10)

POTTERY CANDLE LANTERNS by Bill Dicks
  of Banner Elk, North Carolina
Stoneware clay lanterns in 3 designs: cactus
design with blue/green glaze, flame design with
green glaze, and cattail design with light brown
glaze; specify design; 10" tall with lid.
$23.95 each (3.00)

MIXING BOWL SET by Paul Menchhofer
  of Oak Ridge, Tennessee
Nest of three bowls with spouts; each decorated
with loose swirls in browns and blues; made of
stoneware clay in approximately 1-, 2-, and 3-
quart capacities.
$32.95 set (3.80)

✥

SPOON HOLDER by Tom Seelos
　of Woodstock, Georgia
Earthenware clay body, slip-decorated surface
and lined with satin black glaze, dishwasher
safe, averages 6½" tall with top rim 5¾" diameter.
$14.95 (2.00)

ROLLING PIN by Rude Osolnik
　of Berea, Kentucky
Laminated with Finnish birch, maple, cherry,
walnut, poplar, and mahogany; finished with
non-toxic mineral oil; handles of maple, cherry,
walnut, or poplar. The woods used are identified
on a card with each rolling pin. 17½" long; 2"
diameter.
$32.50 (3.20)

WOODEN SALAD SERVERS by Kentucky Hills
　Industry of Pine Knot, Kentucky
Fork and spoon crafted of native cherry, 13" in
length.
$7.25 pair (.60)

FRENCH TASTING SPOON by Kentucky Hills
　Industry of Pine Knot, Kentucky
Crafted of native cherry and designed to cool the
"taste" as it moves to the sipping end of the
spoon.
$4.50 (.50)

✥

MIRROR by Winthrop Schwab
　of Allisonia, Virginia
Lathe-turned frame of laminated mahogany, 18"
diameter.
$40.00 (4.00)

NECKTIES by Churchill Weavers
　of Berea, Kentucky
All-wool ties in choice of navy, gray, and ginger
heather; 3¼" wide.
$12.00 each (1.00)

SILK SCARVES by Diane Tunkel
　of Knoxville, Tennessee
100% silk scarves batiked with gold swirls, 22"
square.
$17.95 each (1.70)

୧୨

BARK BIRDHOUSE by J. I. Gilliland
 of Horse Shoe, North Carolina
Made of poplar and hickory bark with wood
insert for bottom of house.
$3.95 (1.00)

CARDINAL ON DRIFTWOOD by James Powers
 of Oakdale, Tennessee
Life-sized birds handcarved from basswood,
painted in natural colors in tempera, and
mounted on driftwood.
$25.95 (3.00)

୧୨

ANIMAL MUGS by Carol Sutherland
 of Greenville, South Carolina
White mugs with cobalt decoration; pottery
fired; dishwasher proof, ovenproof, and lead
free; approximately 4" tall, 3" diameter; set of four
with bird, turtle, owl, and rabbit.
$14.95 set (1.70)

BABY BLANKET by Churchill Weavers
 of Berea, Kentucky
White with blocks of soft pastels (pink, blue,
green, and yellow) in plain weave of orlon
acrylic, 36" × 36" with fringed sides.
$18.00 (1.50)

୧୨

CORNSHUCK BOOKMARKS by Lila Marshall
 of Nickelsville, Virginia
"Dollies" made of natural and dyed cornshucks
with cornsilk hair, 6" to 8" long.
$14.95 for six (1.00)

NATURE NOTES by Barbara Hacket,
 Gwen McLaughlin and Helen Ellison
 of Oak Ridge, Tennessee
Handmade parchment-like cover sheet has real
pressed flowers, leaves, and grasses laminated
for protection; in packages of 6 sheets of 4½" ×
5½" note paper, envelopes, and cover sheets.
$6.95 for six (.75)

LOG HAULER by Red Wagon Crafts
of Knoxville, Tennessee
Crafted of poplar or redwood with tiny mimosa
logs, a light oil finish, no splinters or rough
edges, about 7″ × 4½″ × 4½″.
$10.45 (1.50)

CHINESE CHECKERS by Berea College
Student Industries of Berea, Kentucky
Crafted of solid cherry wood, 14″ square, marbles
and instructions included, gift-boxed.
$17.95 (1.75)

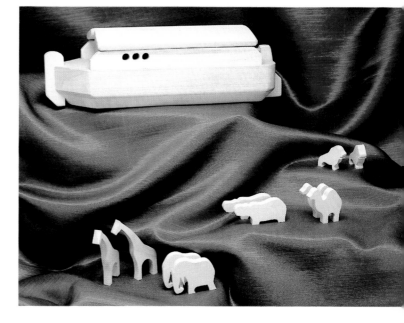

NOAH'S ARK by Yesterday Wooden Toy
Company of Maryville, Tennessee
Constructed of yellow poplar selected for clear
grain; surfaces are hand-sanded. The ark is 18″
long with 5 pairs of animals.
$32.00 (3.75)

TRAPUNTO PILLOWS by Fannie Mennen
 of Rising Fawn, Georgia
Blockprint designs of printer's ink on un-
bleached muslin; sunproof and fadeproof; outer
pillow of linen and cotton blend (undyed) with
separate inner pillow; "Black Oak" and "Turtle"
designs.
$30.00 each (3.00)

TEAPOT WITH CUPS by Michael Sherrill
 of Hendersonville, North Carolina
Salt-glazed stoneware with swirling brushstroke
designs, teapot (approximately 1½-quart capacity) and four cups.
$56.00 set (5.00)

GLASS PAPERWEIGHT by Jak Brewer
 of Zionville, North Carolina
Handblown with an "ice flower" design made of
air bubbles trapped in layers and encased in
transparent glass.
$40.00 (3.25)

CORNSHUCK DOORMAT by Lila Marshall
   of Nickelsville, Virginia
Sturdy, oval doormat braided of natural corn-shucks, 15″ × 24″.
$25.90 (2.50)

MOUNTAIN HEARTH BROOM by Larry Pierson
   of Clinchport, Virginia
Hearth broom with decorative handle, woven of broom corn, selected broom corn fibers, and jute-hemp cord, 40″ to 43″ long.
$18.50 (2.00)

FAWN WISP BROOM by Larry Pierson
   of Clinchport, Virginia
Broom for hearth, work bench, or car, woven of broom corn, dyed fiber, and jute-hemp cord, 12″ to 14″ long.
$5.95 (.50)

STRIPPED HONEYSUCKLE BASKETS by the
   Red Bird Mission of Beverly, Kentucky
Native honeysuckle vines woven over mimosa framework, bark stripped off honeysuckle to reveal the sandy color of the fiber, 10″ diameter.
$26.50 (2.00)

ལྗ

KEROSENE OIL LAMPS by Bob and Angie
   Wagar of Asheville, North Carolina
High-fired stoneware thrown on a potter's wheel, 5″ to 7″ lamp with 10″ hurricane shade; specify blue or brown tones.
$26.95 each (4.00)

HARDWOOD PUZZLE by Robert Brunk
   of Barnardsville, North Carolina
Handcrafted mind teaser of native hardwoods (oak, walnut, cherry, and poplar), puzzle for all ages has forty combinations.
$20.00 (2.00)

LEISURE THROW by Churchill Weavers
   of Berea, Kentucky
Soft blue lap robe in plain weave of all-wool fiber, 50″ × 72″.
$54.00 (3.50)

Eleventh Hour Gifts

Last-minute gifts are just as important as those you purchased months in advance, but even the most conscientious shopper runs out of ideas once in a while. Whether your eleventh-hour shopping "puzzle" is a grandparent or grandchild, best friend or neighbor, paper boy or babysitter, you still want the gift to be just right.

The ideas presented here are elaborate and exciting in appearance, but each is simply a well-thought-out "package" of relatively easy-to-find articles. The impact comes in the way in which you cluster the small items into one big surprise. The gifts are the wrappings, so simply add a big, bright bow and a gift tag.

OVERNIGHT CASE. *Perfect for a favorite granddaughter of any age. It's sure to encourage more weekend visits. Tuck in a fleecy robe, slippers, toothbrush, and a special toy or bedtime story to guarantee sweet dreams. You needn't wrap; just add a luggage tag with the child's name. This idea is easily adapted to a special grandson, and why not stock your teenage granddaughter's first cosmetic case.*

∽∾

SPORTS TOTE. *A collection of equipment and/or accessories for any active boy—or girl. Stuff it with the all-important warm-up jacket and socks. Then add the sports paraphernalia needed with your child's favorite activity. Make it a tennis tote, a soccer bag, or even a clutch of general shape-up equipment as shown here.*

GOURMET COLLECTIONS. *Happy surprises with almost unlimited possibilities. Choose items relating to a particular dish—soufflé, quiche, or, as shown here, a crepe pan with cookbook, whisk, panholder, serving dish, even a striped apron. (You might even tuck in a few of your favorite crepe recipes.) Adapt the selections for a man whose specialty is backyard barbeques. Or give a casserole to hold lasagna, an Italian cookbook, and spices. This is an excellent gift idea for new homemakers.*

SPRINGTIME IN DECEMBER. *A pot of flowers in bloom, bulbs that promise even more color, and a book for dreaming during long winter days. For your vegetable gardener, fill a basket with seed packets and garden row markers. For your friend in an apartment, deliver a lush houseplant and mister or a compact window herb garden or terrarium. For the herb enthusiast, give a collection of seed packets, a booklet on the medicinal values of herbs, and a pair of herb snippers.*

TOOL KITS. *For the men in your life who love working with their hands, get them started with a set of basic carpentry tools, as shown here, or adapt the collection to a particular hobby. For a teenager with his first car, fill an inexpensive tool kit with the very basics in car maintenance tools, including a chamois, turtle wax, etc. For someone just starting out, pack a gift basket of essentials—hammer, picture hangers, nails, screwdriver, pliers, and a tape measure.*

COLLECTIBLE TINS. *Treasures when they're empty or chock full of someone's favorite nuts. (To order nuts, see page 111.) Satisfy a sweet tooth by filling the tins with candy, fudge, or cookies. These are excellent, relatively inexpensive gifts for teachers, neighbors, and good friends. For more personalized "fillings," try the recipes for Homemade Granola (page 98), Toasted Pecans (page 96), and Hot Mocha Mix (page 62).*

Holiday Delights

Specialties from all over the country have been carefully chosen to help you celebrate this Christmas season in style. All orders should be sent directly to the suppliers, who are directly responsible for the quality of their products and service. The special-offer prices of the items in this section are available from September 1, 1981, through January 31, 1982. After January 31, 1982, contact the suppliers to verify prices before ordering.

Baked Goods

HERITAGE BRANDIED APRICOT CAKE—Apricots, pecans, raisins, dates; nothing candied; no preservatives. Packaged for gift giving.

1½ lbs.	$12.00 ppd
3 lbs.	$20.00 ppd

Matthews 1812 House, Whitcomb Hill Road, Box 15, Cornwall Bridge, CT 06754.

FRUITCAKE—1 and 2 lbs. in red leatherette gift box; 3 and 5 lbs. in reusable metal gift tin.

2 lbs.	$15.95 ppd
5 lbs.	$29.95 ppd

Butterfield Farms, Inc., 330 Washington Street, Marina Del Ray, CA 90291.

PECAN CAKE—Includes pecans, dates, cherries, and pineapple. 2-lb. cake in oblong decorative box; 5-lb. cake in decorative tin.

2 lbs.	$9.85 ppd
5 lbs.	$21.50 ppd

Eilenberger's Butter Nut Baking Co., P.O. Box 710, Palestine, TX 75801.

FAMOUS MORAVIAN COOKIES—Specify spice, sugar, or black walnut. Each packaged in decorative red tin.

1 lb.	$11.95 ppd

Moravian Cookie Shop, Inc., 971 Meadowlark Drive, Dept. A, Winston-Salem, NC 27106.

Cheeses

FIVE BIG BARS—One 10-oz. bar of each: Tillamook Natural Cheddar, smoked, sharp, and medium; Tillamook Monterey Jack, very mild; and Tillamook Caraway Spice.

4 lbs.	#88	
East of Rocky Mtns.		$14.50 ppd
West of Rocky Mtns.		$13.20 ppd

Tillamook County Creamery Assn., P.O. Box 313, Tillamook, OR 97141.

HOT PEPPER CHEESE—Processed cheese mixed with hot jalapeño peppers.

2 lbs.	Continental U.S.	$8.95 ppd

Mousetrap Cheese Shop, Box 249, Lewisburg, TN 37091.

BLUE CHEESE—2- and 4-lb. wheels of Maytag Blue Cheese.

2-lb. wheel	$12.00 ppd
4-lb. wheel	$20.00 ppd

Maytag Dairy Farms, P.O. Box 806-S, Newton, IA 50208.

ADOBE PETALUMA—Includes 3-lb. Sonoma Jack wheel, ½ lb. salame, 1 lb. mild cheddar, and 1 lb. Carraway Jack. Packaged and shipped in branded wood box.

5½ lbs.	In California	$26.75 ppd
	Outside California	$32.95 ppd

Sonoma Cheese Factory, 2 Spain Street, Sonoma, CA 95476.

CHEESE GIFT PACK—Gift box contains 1½ lbs. Monterey Jack cheese, 13 oz. Columbus Italian dry salame, and 10 oz. sharp Tillamook

cheese bar. (APO, FPO, and Hawaii add $2 plus $1.75 handling charge.)

1 gift box	$19.95 ppd

San Francisco Bay Gourmet, P.O. Box 1526, Mountain View, CA 94042.

Confections

CARDS OF CHOCOLATE—Milk or dark chocolate card decorated with short message and sold in a wooden gift crate.

Small Card	$23.00 ppd
(6″ × 8″) up to 8 words	
Large Card	$44.00 ppd
(8″ × 16″) up to 12 words	

Krön Chocolatier, 764 Madison Avenue, New York, NY 10021.

FUDGE SAMPLER—Includes Chocolate Walnut, old-fashioned Penuche, real Maple Walnut; and Peanut Butter fudge.

2 lbs.	$9.95 ppd

The Fudge Factory, P.O. Box 1142, Manchester Center, VT 05255.

DELUXE GIFT BOX—8 oz. each of roasted and salted peanuts, chocolate peanut clusters, teejays, peanut crickle, pecan crickle, and roasted and salted pecan halves. (Rocky Mtn. and West Coast States add $2 to price.)

4 lbs.	$16.95 ppd

DeSoto Nut House, P.O. Box 75, DeSoto, GA 31743.

ASSORTED CANDIES—Pralines, divinity, chocolate, vanilla and caramel fudges, caramels, and sugar-coated pecans. Packed in decorative container.

12 oz.	Continental U.S.	$8.25 ppd

Punta Clara Kitchen, Inc., P.O. Box 338, Point Clear, AL 36564.

CREOLE PRALINE SAUCE—Praline syrup with pecans.

2 10-oz. jars	$7.95 ppd

Gazin-Robinson, Inc., P.O. Box 19221, New Orleans, LA 70179.

ASSORTED PRALINES—Ten individually wrapped pralines: rum, chocolate, maple, and original.

10 oz.	**$9.45 ppd**

Evans Creole Candy Co., 848 Decatur Street, New Orleans, LA 70116.

VERMONT MAPLE SYRUP—Pure Vermont grade A maple syrup.

1 qt.	**East of Miss. River**	**$11.15 ppd**
	West of Miss. River	**$11.70 ppd**

Green Mountain Sugar House, RFD 1, Dept. CSL, Ludlow, VT 05149.

Fruits

VERMONT DRIED FRUIT SAMPLER—Contains 1 lb. whole Turkish apricots, 1 lb. tangy apple rings, 1 lb. honey-dipped pineapple, 1 lb. green mountain mix (10 fruits and nuts), and 1 lb. nutty mix.

6 lbs.	**$14.95 ppd**

Sweet Energy, P.O. Box G-1, Essex Center, VT 05451.

ORANGES, GRAPEFRUIT & HONEY—Indian River seedless navel oranges and red grapefruit, plus three 8-oz. jars Florida honey and a honey bear dispenser. (Add $2.50 per package for delivery west of Miss. River.)

25 lbs.	**#3SL**	**$24.50 ppd**

Sullivan Victory Groves, P.O. Box 10, Dept. S, Cocoa, FL 32922.

DATE GIFT PACK—Assortment always includes Medjool and Deglet Noor varieties and four others as available.

4½ lbs.	**#6C**	**$15.75 ppd**

Laflin Date Gardens, P.O. Box 757, Thermal, CA 92274.

GRAPEFRUIT & AVOCADOS—Six Indian River ruby red grapefruit and six buttery smooth avocados packed in a gift box. (Add 10% for delivery west of Miss. River.)

16 lbs.	**#228**	**$19.95 ppd**

Hale Indian River Groves, Dept A232, Wabasso, FL 32970.

JUMBO BONANZA—1 lb. each of dried Blenheim apricots, Freestone peaches, Bartlett pears, and Imperial prunes.

4 lbs.	**Continental U.S.**	**$17.95 ppd**

The Apricot Farm, 2620 Buena Vista Road, Hollister, CA 95023.

ORANGES & GRAPEFRUIT—¼ bushel navel oranges and seedless grapefruit with ½ lb. coconut patties (chocolate-covered candy) included at no extra cost. (No shipments to Alaska, Hawaii or Arizona. Add 10% for delivery west of Miss. River.)

1 order	**$13.75 ppd**

Driftwood Fruit Co., P.O. Box 297, Vero Beach, FL 32960.

CALIFORNIA DRIED FRUIT—Package includes cut apricots, pears, peaches, prunes, and pitted and whole dried apricots. (Alaska and Hawaii add $2 per 3 lbs., $4 per 6 lbs.)

3 lbs.	**$8.75 ppd**
6 lbs.	**$15.95 ppd**

G.I.M.M. Dry Yard, Rt. 1, Box 109-A, Wolfskill Road, Winters, CA 95694.

Meats, Poultry & Seafood

CORNED BEEF BRISKET—Naturally brined corned beef brisket. Specify red or gray (New York style or New England style).

5-6 lbs. avg. wt.	
East of Miss. River	**$16.95 ppd**
West of Miss. River	**$18.95 ppd**
(except Hawaii)	

The Black Rose, 160 State Street, Boston, MA 02109.

HICKORY-SMOKED SAUSAGE—One 2-lb. poke of old-time hickory-smoked pork sausage, seasoned with peppers, sage, and other herbs and spices. (Limit one per person, one-time only. West of Denver add $.50.)

2 lbs.	**$4.95 ppd**

TASTER BOX—One 2-lb. smoked sausage, 1 lb. sugar-cured, hickory-smoked, sliced country bacon, and six slices (8 oz.) salt-cured, aged, red-eye-gravy country ham. (Limit one per person, one-time only. West of Denver add $.50.)

3½ lbs.	**$9.95 ppd**

Early's Honey Stand, RR 2, Dept. OX, Spring Hill, TN 37174.

BACON—Smithfield slab bacon.

4-6 lbs.	**$15.95 ppd**

HAM—Jamestown cooked bone-in ham.

9-12 lbs.	**$43.95 ppd**

Smithfield Packing Co., P.O. Box 447, Smithfield, VA 23430.

COUNTRY HAMS—Federally inspected, aged, and guaranteed.

14-15 lbs. uncooked	**#U4A**	**$47.10 ppd**
9-10 lbs. cooked	**#C9A**	**$51.10 ppd**

PORK SAUSAGE—Grandma Broadbent's smoked country pork sausage.

4.3-4.7 lbs.	**#202A**	**$15.20 ppd**

Broadbent's B & B Food Products, Inc., Rt. 1-SL, Cadiz, KY 42211.

FILET MIGNON—Apple-smoked filet mignon.

2 lbs. (approx.)	**$24.50 ppd**

TURKEY BREAST—Apple-smoked turkey breast.

7-9 lbs. (approx.)	**$37.00 ppd**

Menuchah Farms Smokehouse, Rt. 22, Salem, NY 12865.

WHOLE TURKEYS—Hickory-smoked whole turkeys. (Ground shipping west of Miss. River add $4. Airmail shipping west of Miss. River add $6.)

9-10 lbs.	**$27.00 ppd**
10-11 lbs.	**$29.50 ppd**

Stegall Smoked Turkey, Inc., 213 Marshville Boulevard, Marshville, NC 28103.

SMOKED SALMON—Whole side of Irish smoked salmon.

over 2 lbs.	**$50.00 ppd**

Caviateria, Inc., 870 Madison Avenue, New York, NY 10021.

LIVE MAINE LOBSTERS—Six lobsters (1 lb. avg.) per order, shipped in ice and seaweed.

	$69.00 ppd

Dark Harbor Lobster Co., P.O. Box 406, Belfast, ME 04915.

Nuts

PISTACHIO NUTS—Packaged in burlap bag.

1 lb.	**$12.00 ppd**

Butterfield Farms, Inc., 330 Washington Street, Marina Del Ray, CA 90291.

DELUXE NUT SAMPLER—Includes 1 lb. 5-crown natural pistachios, 1 lb. golden roasted cashews, 1 lb. mixed nuts.

3 lbs.	**$23.95 ppd**

Sweet Energy, P.O. Box G-1, Essex Center, VT 05451.

---

continued

PECAN HALVES—Mammoth shelled pecan halves.

2½ lbs.	**$15.00 ppd**
5 lbs.	**$27.00 ppd**
10 lbs.	**$52.00 ppd**

Sternberg Pecan Co., P.O. Box 193, Jackson, MS 39205.

PECAN GIFT BOX—Christmas poinsettia-design gift box filled with select pecans. (West of Denver add $.45 per box.)

1½ lbs.	**$9.95 ppd**

B & B Pecan Co., Rt. 2, Box 195, Fairhope, AL 36532.

WATER-BLANCHED PEANUTS—Extra large Virginia water-blanched peanuts cooked in peanut oil. No preservatives or additives. (Add $1 per address west of Miss. River. Virginia residents add 4% tax.)

2½-lb. tin	**$7.85 ppd**
22-oz. tin	**$5.35 ppd**

The Peanut Shop of Williamsburg, P.O. Box GN, Dept. SL, Williamsburg, VA 23185.

MAMMOTH PECAN HALVES—Fancy mammoth pecan halves packed twelve 1-lb. cello bags per case. (Add $2.50 per case if west of Miss. River.)

12 lbs.	**$60.00 ppd**

Sunny South Pecan Co., Box 192, Statesboro, GA 30458.

Specialties

PEPPER JELLY—Three ½ pts. of pepper jelly, a blend of green peppers and red hot peppers.

24 fl. oz.	**Continental U.S.**	**$12.25 ppd**

Punta Clara Kitchen, P.O. Box 338, Point Clear, AL 36564.

CASPION STURGEON CAVIAR—Three 1-oz. jars.

3 oz.	**$20.00 ppd**

AMERICAN STURGEON CAVIAR—Three 1-oz. jars.

3 oz.	**$25.00 ppd**

Caviateria, Inc., 870 Madison Avenue, New York, NY 10021.

HOMEMADE PRESERVES—Gift pack of six 1-pt. jars. Flavors include pineapple, pineapple cherry, pineapple coconut, pineapple mango, pineapple orange, and pineapple strawberry. (Add $2 for shipping west of Miss. River.)

1 gift pack	**$18.00 ppd**

Plantation Paradise, Rt. 3, Box 175, Lake Placid, FL 33852.

NEW ORLEANS BLEND COFFEE—Special blend of coffee and French chicory, vacuum sealed.

3 lbs.	**$9.99 ppd**

Community Coffee Co., Inc., P.O. Box 791, Dept. S, Baton Rouge, LA 70821.

ESCARGOTS—Two dozen per 7-oz. can.

6-can carton	**$16.00 ppd**

ESCARGOTS SHELLS—Two dozen per box.

2 doz.	**$9.00 ppd**

J & K Trading Co., 10808 Garland Drive, Culver City, CA 90230.

TASTES OF CURRY—Gift box of three different curry sauces: curry sauce for meat, saffron-cream curry, and curry sauce for seafood and poultry.

3 10-oz. cans	**$8.90 ppd**

Gourmail, Inc., P.O. Box 853-S, Crosby, TX 77532.

MULLED WINE & CIDER SPICE—Each gift container holds four hand-tied spice balls, enough spice to make 2½ gals. wine or cider.

2.2 oz.	**$5.50 ppd**

The Spice Hunter, Antler Drive, Rt. 2, Box 666-F, Arroyo Grande, CA 93420.

Garlands & Wreaths

RED CHILI PEPPER WREATH—17″ in diameter, approx. 200 peppers. The pepper pods are an edible vegetable product. A book of recipes is included.

1 wreath	**Continental U.S.**	**$17.95 ppd**

WHEAT STRAW WREATH—13″ wreath made from wheat straw with two bells, also fashioned from straw. Tarascan Indian work from Lake Patzcuaro, Mexico.

1 wreath	**Continental U.S.**	**$9.50 ppd**

The Old Mexico Shop, Patio 101, Santa Fe, NM 87501.

HERBAL WREATH—16″ wreath with statice and artemisia base, decorated with cinnamon sticks, nutmegs, gum burrs, red cayenne peppers, red and yellow yarrow, star flowers, safflower, yellow everlastings, eucalyptus, sage, rosemary, thyme, bay, and oregano.

3 lbs.	**Continental U.S.**	**$32.95 ppd**

Gilberties Herb Gardens, Sylvan Avenue, Westport, CT 06880.

CEDAR GARLANDS—7′ long handcrafted garlands are made of freshly cut western red cedar. (For Alaska and Hawaii add $3.50.)

6 lbs.	**$8.50 ppd**

Christmas Forest, 445 Beaver Creek Road, Curtis, WA 98538.

CONE WREATH—This 15″ cone wreath is made up of Ponderosa, Pinyon, Lodgepole Pine, Spruce, Hemlock, Larch, Sequoia, and Redwood cones, plus pods and nuts.

4½ lbs.	**$29.75 ppd**

Gloria's Cone Tree, 42664 Upper Calapooia, Sweet Home, OR 97386.

LONGLEAF PINE CONES—Twenty-five large cones from 5″-8″ long and 3″-4″ in diameter.

1 bu. East of Miss. River only	**$6.00 ppd**

FIREPLACE CONES—Selection of longleaf, slash, loblolly, and white pine for fireplace decorations or burning.

1 bu. East of Miss. River only	**$7.50 ppd**

Land of the Sky Nursery, 108 Lakewood Drive, Asheville, NC 28803.

CEDAR, HERBS & FLOWERS—A blend of herbs, spices, and cedar needles (also available in "Christmas Tree" bags).

4-oz. bags	**$4.00 ppd**
8-oz. bags	**$8.00 ppd**

Clear Light Cedar Co., Placitas, NM 87043.

EDITOR'S NOTE
Any questions concerning the products or services offered in "Holiday Delights" should be directed to the supplier whose address is given. Should you encounter any difficulty, please contact *Southern Living®* Christmas Editor, P.O. Box 2262, Birmingham, AL 35201.

Christmas around the South

The South offers a wealth of adventure to holiday travelers—from the rich Moravian festivities of Old Salem, North Carolina, to the colorful boat parade in Pompano Beach, Florida. "Christmas around the South," a state-by-state guide to holiday events in each of the 16 southern states, describes a variety of activities, some perhaps five states away and some just around the corner in your own hometown. (Dates and contacts are given for each event and it would be wise to check with local sponsors before driving long distances.)

The spirit and gaiety of today's holiday celebrations mingle with the traditions and customs of America's founding fathers. In San Antonio, for example, the *Los Pasados*, a symbolic procession of candlelight and music depicting Mary and Joseph seeking shelter, proceeds solemnly down the *Paseo del Rio* one moment. The next moment the Mexican Marketplace is magically transformed as the *Fiesta Navideña* gets underway with revelers

sampling traditional Mexican pastries and children gleefully attacking a colorful *piñata*.

In this catalogue of southern Christmases, music-lovers find the South literally breaks into song as the holiday season begins. Carols fill the air from Atlanta to the giant Singing Christmas Tree in Antlers, Oklahoma. A Festival of Sacred Music in Birmingham showcases an evening of star-laden entertainment, and thousands of people join in singing carols in New Orleans's Jackson Square. And in Virginia, the haunting music of bagpipes stirs memories of Christmases past in "A Scottish Christmas in Alexandria."

Discover the South in December with the aid of "Christmas around the South" and make your 1981 holiday season not just a pleasant memory, but a memorable adventure.

Alabama

FESTIVAL OF SACRED MUSIC—Birmingham, Alabama. With night performances November 25-28 and a matinee on November 29, a special festival of Christmas music will be held in the Concert Hall of the Birmingham-Jefferson Civic Center. Music will be provided by the Birmingham Symphony Orchestra and Birmingham Civic Chorus, and personalities from the Lawrence Welk Show will be present. Contact: Public Affairs Department, *The Birmingham News*, P.O. Box 2553, Birmingham, Alabama 35202.

OLD-FASHIONED CHRISTMAS AT ARLINGTON—Birmingham, Alabama. December 12-13, this historic home will be decorated in the authentic atmosphere of the nineteenth century, with hostesses dressed in period costumes. The theme will be "A Child's Christmas." Open Saturday, 10 a.m. to 4:30 p.m.; Sunday, 12 noon to 4:30 p.m. Contact: Miss Bryding Adams, Director, Arlington, 331 Cotton Avenue, S.W., Birmingham, Alabama 35211.

CANDLELIGHT CHRISTMAS AT OAKLEIGH—Mobile, Alabama. December 5-6, this historic home will be beautifully decorated as it was in the period just before 1850. Contact: Mrs. Havadna Becker, Historic Mobile Preservation Society, 350 Oakleigh Place, Mobile, Alabama 36604.

A CHRISTMAS PAST AT THE ORDEMAN-SHAW HISTORIC HOME—Montgomery, Alabama. This beautiful home in the Old North Hull Historic District will be decorated in the style of the Victorian yuletide. Open 7 days a week, closed Christmas Day. Contact: Mary Ann Neeley, Landmarks Foundation of Montgomery, 310 North Hull Street, Montgomery, Alabama 36104.

TOUR OF GAINESWOOD—Demopolis, Alabama. On December 3, this beautiful antebellum mansion will be decorated for Christmas as it was in the period before the War Between the States. Period music and chorale groups are also featured. Contact: Gaineswood, 805 Cedar Street, Demopolis, Alabama 36732.

CHRISTMAS IN THE CANE-BRAKE—Demopolis, Alabama. December 5, Bluff Hall, built in 1832, will be decorated with traditional Christmas greenery, fruits, and candlelight. Contact: Mrs. Ben George, Marengo County Historical Society, Box 159, Demopolis, Alabama 36732.

CHRISTMAS AT MAGNOLIA GROVE—Greensboro, Alabama. This beautiful, historic home will be decorated for Christmas as it was when it was built in 1840. Tours on December 13, from 2-5 p.m. Contact: Jack Stell, Alabama Historical Commission, 725 Monroe Street, Montgomery, Alabama 36130.

OLD DECATUR CHRISTMAS CANDLELIGHT TOUR—Decatur, Alabama. This driving or walking tour through a Victorian neighborhood of Old Decatur covers approximately 25 blocks and includes tours of about 22 homes; streets and walks will be lined with over 10,000 candles. December 21-23, from 6-9 p.m. each evening. Contact: Old Decatur Association, 604 Line Street, N.E., Decatur, Alabama 35601.

Arkansas

CHRISTMAS CONCERT—Hot Springs National Park. To be held at the Convention Auditorium December 6 at 3 p.m., the concert will feature three choirs in the musical *Noel Jesus is Born.* Contact: Chamber of Commerce, Convention Auditorium, P.O. Box 1500, Hot Springs National Park, Arkansas 71901.

OPEN HOUSE AT ARKANSAS TERRITORIAL RESTORATION—Little Rock, Arkansas. December 5 and 6, traditional decorations are presented in three different buildings to reflect the historical celebrations of three segments of the territorial society. Contact: Bill Worthen, Arkansas Territorial Restoration, Third and Scott Streets, Little Rock, Arkansas 72201.

Delaware

YULETIDE AT WINTERTHUR—Winterthur, Delaware. November 24-January 3, the yuletide tour will feature visits to rooms decorated in the manner of the period of the house (1640-1840). Contact: Reservations Office, Winterthur Museum and Gardens, Winterthur, Delaware 19735.

A HOLIDAY VISIT TO ELEUTHERIAN MILLS—Wilmington, Delaware. Eleutherian Mills, built in 1802-1803 by E. I. du Pont, will offer seasonal decorations that enhance the furnishings and collections reminiscent of five generations of du Ponts who lived there. Daytime tours: December 4-January 3; evening tours by reservation only. Contact: Candlelight Tour, The Hagley Museum, Box 3630, Greenville, Wilmington, Delaware 19807.

NEW CASTLE HOMES TOURS—New Castle, Delaware. A town of the 1650s, New Castle has within three blocks the George Read II House (Late Georgian 1797-1804), the Anstel House (Early Georgian 1730s), and the Old Dutch House (1690s) as well as the Presbyterian Church (1707), each decorated as it might have been at the time it was built. Candlelight tours will be held December 12-13 and 18-20. Contact: Pamela Swain, Site Administrator, George Read II House, P.O. Box 204, New Castle, Delaware 19720.

Florida

DELAND BOAT PAGEANT—Deland, Florida. December 12, the citizens will deck their boats in Christmas lights and engage in a festive night parade on the St. Johns River from Lake Beresford to Crows Bluff and back. Whitehair Bridge in Deland is the best vantage point from which to view the approximately 38 brightly decorated boats, ranging in length from 16 to 62 feet. Contact: Boat Parade Chairman, c/o Crows Bluff Marina, Deland, Florida 32720.

FORT LAUDERDALE BOAT PARADE—Fort Lauderdale, Florida. December 19, the people of Fort Lauderdale will decorate their crafts and celebrate Christmas by cruising

FORT LAUDERDALE BOAT PARADE—Fort Lauderdale, Florida.

10 miles up the Intracoastal Waterway in a nighttime aquatic parade. Contact: Diane Butler, Chamber of Commerce, Box 14516, Fort Lauderdale, Florida 33302.

MADEIRA BEACH PARADE—Madeira Beach, Florida. December 19, residents will decorate their boats for a colorful parade on Boca Ciega near St. Petersburg. Contact: The City Manager, City of Madeira Beach, 300 Municipal Drive, Madeira Beach, Florida 33708.

CHRISTMAS BOAT PARADE—Pompano Beach, Florida. The first parade of its kind and the oldest in the nation will be held this year on December 20. Over 100 boats, decorated with gaily colored lights and bearing carolers, cruise the Intracoastal Waterway. Contact: Greater Pompano Beach Chamber of Commerce, 2200 East Atlantic Boulevard, Pompano Beach, Florida 33062.

Georgia

CHRISTMAS AROUND THE WORLD—Macon, Georgia. November 22 through the end of the year, the Museum of Arts and Sciences will offer its popular annual Christmas exhibit. The exhibit will feature the themes of the Music of Christmas, Colonial Christmas at Williamsburg, and Christmas Trees of the World. The museum's Mark Smith Planetarium presents "The Star of Bethlehem," which seeks to offer scientific explanations of what that mysterious object in the sky that guided the Wise Men to Bethlehem might have been. Contact: Mr. David Eldridge, Director, The Museum of Arts and Sciences, 4182 Forsyth Road, Macon, Georgia 31210.

ANNUAL LIVING NATIVITY PAGEANT—Stone Mountain, Georgia. December 15-18 at 7:30 p.m, a narrated drama of the birth of Christ will be portrayed on Memorial Plaza lawn with a cast of Atlanta area young people, live animals, lights, and music. To watch the free pageant, visitors may relax on the sloping five-acre lawn that provides a natural amphitheater in front of the Stone Mountain carving. Contact: Kathi Hayes, Public Relations Dept., Stone Mountain Park, P.O. Box 778, Stone Mountain, Georgia 30086.

CALLAWAY GARDENS' CHRISTMAS—Pine Mountain, Georgia. Callaway Gardens will celebrate Christmas with holiday festivities which will include nature walks, craftsmen demonstrating and teaching their talents, tree trimming, special horticultural workshops, and candy-making classes.

THE NUTCRACKER ballet (shown here in Atlanta) is presented in many cities.

The festivities will be kicked off with a Madrigal Dinner in the tradition of Olde England, and the merrymaking will end with the New Year's Eve dinner dance. Contact: Christmas at Callaway Gardens, Pine Mountain, Georgia 31822.

TULLIE SMITH HOUSE—Atlanta, Georgia. On December 16 and 17, candlelight tours will include music and caroling, demonstrations of nineteenth-century crafts (spinning, weaving, quilting, making samplers), and refreshments of malt cider and gingersnaps that are cooked on the open hearth. Contact: Margaret Brock, Director, Atlanta Historical Society, 3099 Andrews Drive, N.W., Atlanta, Georgia 30305.

HOLIDAY CEREMONIES OF WESTVILLE—Lumpkin, Georgia. In this restored village of the 1850s, the yule season extends from December 12-26 (closed Christmas Day). The village is decorated in eighteenth- and nineteenth-century fashion. Each Saturday, a special activity is planned. Contact: Mack Moye, Westville, P.O. Box 1850, Lumpkin, Georgia 31815.

Kentucky

LIVING NATIVITY—Bethlehem, Kentucky. On December 22-25, 6:30 to 9 p.m., the Nativity scene will be presented, with characters wearing authentic dress and live animals adding to the realism. Contact: Alvin L. Roberts, Bethlehem Living Nativity, Bethlehem, Kentucky 40007.

CHRISTMAS FESTIVAL—Natchitoches, Louisiana.

and the procession into the square will begin with thousands of voices singing Christmas carols. Contact: John Bogie, 7216 Zimple, New Orleans, Louisiana 70118.

HODGES GARDENS' CHRISTMAS LIGHTS—Many, Louisiana. December 4-23, multicolored lights around the shore of the gardens' 220-acre lake illuminate the scene for the festival. Larger-than-life papier-mâché figures, arrayed in colorful robes, realistically depict the Holy Land of long ago. Admission is free from 5 p.m. to 9 p.m. Contact: Carol Vinson, Publicity Director, Hodges Gardens, P.O. Box 921, Many, Louisiana 71449.

CHRISTMAS FESTIVAL—Natchitoches, Louisiana. December 5, this 260-year-old town, the oldest in the Louisiana Purchase territory, will stage a show that includes a parade down Front Street, entertainment on a river-bank stage, an elaborate fireworks display, and the turning on of the Christmas lights throughout the town. Contact: Natchitoches Parish Chamber of Commerce, P.O. Box 3, Natchitoches, Louisiana 71457.

Louisiana

CHRISTMAS EVE BONFIRE CELEBRATION—Lutcher-Gramercy area along River Road, between New Orleans and Baton Rouge, Louisiana. Beginning October 24, citizens will build more than one hundred 30-foot-tall pyramid-shaped bonfires along the river. On Christmas Eve, the bonfires will be lit and burn into the night. Rockets, sparklers, and other fireworks add

to the gaiety of the spectacular affair. Contact: Louisiana Tourist Commission, P.O. Box 44291, Baton Rouge, Louisiana 70804.

PATIO PLANTERS' CHRISTMAS CAROL CELEBRATION—New Orleans, Louisiana. December 20, guests will assemble at 6:30 p.m. at each of the four gates into Jackson Square. As the St. Louis Cathedral bells toll 7 p.m., candles will be lit

Maryland

CHRISTMAS AT MOUNT CLARE—Baltimore, Maryland. December 12 and 13, this museum house of eighteenth-century furnishings will be decorated with Christmas arrangements in the Colonial manner. Programs of eighteenth-century music (recorder, harpsichord, choral) are planned. Contact: Mount Clare, Carroll Park, Baltimore, Maryland 21230.

CHRISTMAS TREE—Washington, D.C.

COLONIAL CHRISTMAS AT HAM-MOND-HARWOOD HOUSE—Annapolis, Maryland. Around the middle of December, this beautiful Georgian mansion will be decorated as it was in the eighteenth century. A greens sale will be conducted in addition to a candlelight tour of the house by hostesses in authentic costume. Contact: Administrator, The Hammond-Harwood House, 19 Maryland Avenue, Annapolis, Maryland 21401.

CHRISTMAS OPEN HOUSE AND BAZAAR AT CARROLL COUNTY FARM MUSEUM—Westminster, Maryland. The weekend of Thanksgiving, the Gift Shoppe will be filled with numerous Christmas gift ideas. December 5 and 6, the Main House will be decorated as it was in the nineteenth century. On December 6 at 6 p.m., a Friendship Candle Lighting Service will be held, along with a community carol sing. Contact: Cindy Hofferberth, Director, Carroll County Farm Museum, Westminster, Maryland 21157.

VICTORIAN CHRISTMAS AT MILLER HOUSE—Hagerstown, Maryland. December 15-31 (closed Mondays and Christmas Day), the historic Miller House will be decorated as it was in days gone by. Special exhibits in the various rooms of the house will include three trees depicting various eras. Contact: Mrs. Kenneth Peters, 135 W. Washington, Hagerstown, Maryland 21740.

Mississippi

TREES OF CHRISTMAS TOUR AT MERREHOPE—Meridian, Mississippi. December 4-13, this historic Mississippi home will feature live 12-foot trees with varying decorations in every room. A craft show will also feature many handmade ornaments and gifts for sale. Contact: Merrehope, 905 31st Avenue, Meridian, Mississippi 39301.

CHRISTMAS PAGEANT—Leland, Mississippi. From December 8 until January 1, Deer Creek, which runs through the Delta town of Leland, will come alive with floats depicting the spirit of Christmas. December 8, children can await the arrival of Santa Claus on a gaily decorated float. Contact: Leland Chamber of Commerce, P.O. Box 67, Leland, Mississippi 38756.

CHRISTMAS HOMES TOUR—McComb, Mississippi. The afternoon of December 6, two homes in the McComb area will be tastefully and artistically decorated according to the style of the homes. Contact: Mrs. David Feldman, 509 Laurel Street, Summit, Mississippi 39666.

North Carolina

WORLD'S LARGEST LIVING CHRISTMAS TREE—Wilmington, North Carolina. December 11, the lights will be illuminated on a large water oak, 75 feet tall with a limb spread of 210 feet. The town claims it to be the world's largest living Christmas tree. It is traditionally draped with 5 tons of Spanish moss and lighted by over 4,500 multicolored lights. Contact: Greater Wilmington Chamber of Commerce, P.O. Box 330, Wilmington, North Carolina 28402.

OLD WILMINGTON BY CANDLE-LIGHT—Wilmington, North Carolina. December 12 and 13, the warmth and charm of historic Wilmington is experienced during this tour by the opening of several gracious homes and churches. Contact: James R. Warren, Chairman, P.O. Box 813, Wilmington, North Carolina 28402.

SALEM CHRISTMAS—Winston-Salem, North Carolina. December 15, the sights, sounds, and smells of Christmastime long ago will be recreated in the restored Moravian town of Old Salem. Visitors may walk through the historic area and enjoy the unhurried, warm-hearted atmosphere of the town as it was nearly 200 years ago. In the restored buildings of the town, activities typical of Salem in the 1800s are recreated. Traditional Christmas music is provided by roving bands. Contact: Department of Information, Old Salem, Inc., Drawer F, Salem Station, Winston-Salem, North Carolina 27108.

SALEM CHRISTMAS—Winston-Salem, North Carolina.

SINGING TREE—Charlotte, North Carolina.

SINGING CHRISTMAS TREE—Charlotte, North Carolina. December 11-13, a giant tree with hundreds of shining lights will gradually glow from soft light to a brilliant splendor. The music will be by the Charlotte Choral Society. The theme of the show will be depicted with beautiful sets, costumed dancers, and musical selections. An appearance by Santa and falling snow on stage will highlight the occasion. Contact: The Charlotte Choral Society, Spirit Square, 110 E. 7th Street, Charlotte, North Carolina 28202.

Oklahoma

SINGING CHRISTMAS TREE—Antlers, Oklahoma. Each night from 8 to 9 p.m., December 20-24, some 125 choir members, robed in white and standing on steps in the shape of a tree, form the "singing Christmas tree." It is located off the Indian Nation Turnpike where parking is available for some 2,500 cars. Contact: Rev. H. L. Morrison, Box 336, Antlers, Oklahoma 74523.

OLD-FASHIONED CHRISTMAS AT THE OLD TOWN MUSEUM—Elk City, Oklahoma. At 2 p.m. on December 6, a tree will be placed in the gazebo on the grounds of the museum, an authentic western Oklahoma home built at the turn of the century and furnished with Victorian furniture. It is decorated with green garlands and red bows and ornaments. Carols will be sung, candy passed out, and a puppet show presented, followed by Santa Claus's timely visit. Contact: Curator, Old Town Museum, P.O. Box 542, Elk City, Oklahoma 73648.

South Carolina

CHRISTMAS IN CHARLESTON—Charleston, South Carolina. The whole month of December will see the business and historic districts filled with singing groups, beautifully decorated museum mansion houses, and historic churches decorated for the holidays. Christmas concerts, ballets, and plays will be presented. December 12, a Christmas parade of boats is featured at night in Charleston Harbor. Contact: Christmas in Charleston, P.O. Box 975, Charleston, South Carolina 29402.

JOSEPH MANIGAULT HOUSE—Charleston, South Carolina. December 5 and 6, this Adam-style mansion, completed about 1803, will be decorated by the Garden Club of Charleston. Native materials are used and the house is lit with candles in the late afternoon. Sweetgrass ornaments are fashioned by local basket makers; small baskets, stars, and kissing balls can be purchased. Contact: Manigault House, 137 Broad Street, Charleston, South Carolina 29401.

CHRISTMAS AT THE VERDIER HOUSE—Beaufort, South Carolina. A week-long open house, December 7-12, features decorations consistent with this Federal-style house with furnishings of the period of its construction, *circa* 1790. Contact: Verdier House, P.O. Box 11, Beaufort, South Carolina 29902.

Tennessee

NATIVITY PAGEANT—Knoxville, Tennessee. December 13-15, a cast of 84 local actors, live animals, and a 175-voice choir will present a pageant of the Nativity. Contact: Mrs. George Harrison, P.O. Box 10871, Knoxville, Tennessee 37919.

THE TREES OF CHRISTMAS AT CHEEKWOOD—Nashville, Tennessee. For three weeks, beginning on December 5, a display of 19 trees at the Tennessee Botanical Gardens and Fine Arts Center will include those decorated in the tradition of seven or eight countries as well as novelty trees such as the "Sugarplum Fairy Tree." Also on hand will be a display of handicrafts. Contact: The Tennessee Botanical Gardens and Fine Arts Center, Inc., Cheekwood Road, Nashville, Tennessee 37205.

A DICKENS CHRISTMAS—Memphis, Tennessee. December 3-23, every night except Monday, two performances on Sunday. "A Christmas Carol" will be produced by Theatre Memphis, one of the oldest and largest community theaters in the country. Contact: Theatre Memphis, 630 Perkins Ext., Memphis, Tennessee 38117.

CANDLELIGHT TOUR OF CARTER HOUSE—Franklin, Tennessee. December 5 and 6, 5 to 9 p.m. This large farmhouse, built in 1828, served as the union headquarters during the Battle of Franklin in November 1864. Furnished in the period of the early 1800s, the house is decorated to reflect the period. Contact: Carter House, 1140 Columbia Avenue, Franklin, Tennessee 37064.

FESTIVAL OF TREES—Gatlinburg, Tennessee. December 3-13, in the civic auditorium, various trees are decorated in different themes and motifs, depicting trees from different parts of the world. Contact: Chamber of Commerce, P.O. Box 527, Gatlinburg, Tennessee 37738.

CHRISTMAS CELEBRATIONS—San Antonio, Texas.

CHRISTMAS CELEBRATION—San Antonio, Texas. Beginning December 1 and continuing throughout the season, the Holiday River Festival will feature barges with choirs traveling along the San Antonio River between trees strung with lights. Special events will include the *Fiesta de Las Luminarias* (festival of lights) December 11-13; *Las Pasados* (Joseph and Mary seeking shelter) December 13; and the *Fiesta Navideña* (traditional Mexican activities including a *piñata* party for children and the blessing of the animals). Contact: San Antonio Convention and Visitors Bureau, P.O. Box 2277, San Antonio, Texas 78298.

LOS PASTORES—San Antonio, Texas. On December 26 and 27 at the San José Mission, an old, primitive pageant depicting the birth of Christ will be presented. Contact: San Antonio Conservation Society, 107 King William Street, San Antonio, Texas 78204.

POINSETTIA SHOW—Mission, Texas. In the second week in December, Mission, Texas, will remind the Rio Grande Valley of the advent of the Christmas season with a display of the beautiful and traditional Christmas flower in the only all-poinsettia show in the nation. Contact: Mrs. T. L. Duncan, Box 706, Mission, Texas 78572.

MIDWESTERN-BURNS FANTASY OF LIGHTS—Wichita Falls, Texas. Four of the campus buildings of Midwestern State University each year are decorated with some 12,000 red, white, and yellow bulbs. These and over 30 Christmas exhibits, many of which are animated, form the "Fantasy of Lights." They will be turned on December 4 and shine throughout the holiday season. Contact: Mr. Steve Holland, Midwestern State University, 3400 Taft Street, Wichita Falls, Texas 76308.

DICKENS'S EVENING ON THE STRAND—Galveston, Texas. December 5, this unique yuletide celebration (named Texas's most outstanding winter event) re-creates a "living" Victorian street scene in the Historic Strand District. Dickens's Scrooge, Tiny Tim, Oliver Twist, and a host of others come to life among strolling carolers, musicians, dancers, and vendors selling dancing dolls and roasted chestnuts. More than 100 Victorian "shoppes" are housed in nineteenth-century buildings and open-air marketplaces. Contact: Galveston Historical Foundation, P.O. Drawer 539, Galveston, Texas 77553.

THE GLOW OF CHRISTMAS—Galveston, Texas. Ashton Villa, an 1859 restored Galveston mansion, will be elaborately decorated inside and out with traditional Victorian holiday splendor and open free to the public December 13-15, from 6 to 8 p.m. From 5 to 6 p.m. on December 15, the mansion will open to special guests in wheelchairs and the elderly. A dozen or more choirs will perform Christmas carols, and volunteers will be dressed as Victorian family members. Contact: Judy Schiebel, Ashton Villa, P.O. Box 1616, Galveston, Texas 77553.

Virginia

CHRISTMAS WALK—Alexandria, Virginia. "A Scottish Christmas in Alexandria" emphasizes the Scottish origin of this historic city with bagpipe bands providing stirring music, a special Scottish Advent Service, tours of decorated historic homes, a special "Wonderful World" for children, a display of early firefighting equipment, plus sales of Christmas greens, antiques, and taste-tempting goodies. Contact: Christmas Walk, 418 South Washington Street, Alexandria, Virginia 22314.

CHRISTMAS WALK—Alexandria, Virginia.

CHRISTMAS CANDLELIGHT WALKING TOUR—Fredericksburg, Virginia. On December 6, costumed hostesses, horse-drawn carriage rides, Christmas greens, carolers, and candlelit homes will welcome visitors to Fredericksburg's oldest and most elegant neighborhoods. Contact: Historic Fredericksburg Foundation, 623 Caroline Street, Fredericksburg, Virginia 22401.

CHRISTMAS IN WILLIAMSBURG—Williamsburg, Virginia. December 16-January 1, this Christmas program will present a fortnight of traditional and Colonial activities featuring dramatic lighting, games, feasting, and special events. Contact: Colonial Williamsburg Foundation, P.O. Box B, Williamsburg, Virginia 23185.

CAROLS BY CANDLELIGHT AT GUNSTON HALL PLANTATION—Lorton, Virginia. December 11-13, a tour will be given of this historic plantation built in 1755 by George Mason and decorated in the eighteenth-century manner. Music and caroling will be a part of the celebration. Contact: Gunston Hall Plantation, Lorton, Virginia 22079.

THE NATIVITY—Richmond, Virginia. This outdoor pageant will be held Christmas Eve at 6 p.m. at the Carillon in Byrd Park. The story of the Nativity will be done in pantomime with narration and music, featuring a cast of 250 and a choir of 100. Contact: Department of Recreation and Parks, City of Richmond, 900 East Broad Street, Richmond, Virginia 23219.

West Virginia

OLD-FASHIONED CHRISTMAS—Harpers Ferry, West Virginia. December 4-6, visitors can take a candlelight walk through the streets of Harpers Ferry. Shops will be lighted by candles, and the streets, by old-fashioned lamps. Carolers and roving musicians will provide the music. Contact: D. D. Kilham, Hilltop House Hotel, Harpers Ferry, West Virginia 25425.

Christmas Journal

hristmas, when it is still in the future, is a specific date—a day when all the gifts will have been chosen, the food prepared, the family gathered, and the celebration begun. Christmas, when it is in the past, is a feeling—a blending and blurring of all our memories into a very private definition of just what the day means.

This "Christmas Journal" is designed as an aid to both plan and memory. We select tangible gifts to express the intangibles of love and sharing, and we open our homes and ourselves to the observance of this season of abundance. All this activity, though, requires preparation and organization—there are gifts to buy, goodies to bake, cards to mail, and parties to plan. Specific lists for gifts, sizes, cards, and activities are clustered in this section so that you have, all in one place, a planning guide for your preparations and scheduling. After the holidays, these same lists, now completed, will remind you of the many pleasures of the season.

November and December calendars will help you prepare for Christmas 1981. Use the calendars as an appointment diary for recording parties or meetings and for scheduling time to participate in some of the many community activities of the season. Browse through the chapter entitled "Christmas around the South" to help plan your holiday adventure.

Additional pages are left for you to make an album of the season—pages for photographs to save the moments of pleasure when a child decorates the first sugar cookie, when a long-awaited present is opened, when someone special joins the family circle. Keep a camera and this journal handy as you revel in the Christmas season, and record, in snapshots as well as in lists of gifts and events, the preparations and the happy results.

Gift List

Gift lists are a must at Christmastime. By filling in the blanks as you complete your shopping, you can see at a glance what you have accomplished and what you have yet to do.

To avoid revealing any secrets, you may prefer to use this page as a "wish" list—a record of items for which various family members have expressed a desire. Whichever way you use this handy organizer, the lists will become part of your Christmas memory—a reminder of what helped to make 1981 a very special holiday.

Name

gifts:

stocking stuffers:

Name

gifts:

stocking stuffers:

Name

gifts:

stocking stuffers:

Name

gifts:

stocking stuffers:

Name

gifts:

stocking stuffers:

Name

gifts:

stocking stuffers:

Relatives & Friends

Size Charts

Name _____

gift: _____

Name _____

gift: _____

Name _____

gift: _____

Name _____

gift: _____

Name _____

gift: _____

Name _____

gift: _____

Name _____

gift: _____

Name _____

gift: _____

How do you ask someone's size without revealing what you intend the gift to be? Simply fill in one of the size charts below for each member of your family. Be sure to indicate "types" of sizes, such as petite, misses, junior, half-sizes, small, medium, large, extra-large, slim, chubby, etc. A quick peek at this page will eliminate much of the guessing involved when your family shops for clothing gifts.

Name		Name	
height	weight	height	weight
coat	slacks	coat	slacks
dress	pajamas	dress	pajamas
suit	bathrobe	suit	bathrobe
sweater	shoes	sweater	shoes
shirt	hat	shirt	hat
blouse	gloves	blouse	gloves
skirt	ring	skirt	ring

Name		Name	
height	weight	height	weight
coat	slacks	coat	slacks
dress	pajamas	dress	pajamas
suit	bathrobe	suit	bathrobe
sweater	shoes	sweater	shoes
shirt	hat	shirt	hat
blouse	gloves	blouse	gloves
skirt	ring	skirt	ring

Holiday Schedule

Different family members belong to different groups, and it seems that every group plans a celebration of the season. Arrangements must be made for everything from adults' formal parties to buying a bag of potato chips for the pre-schooler's play group party. Some parties require gifts for friends or for charitable purposes.

Here, to help you keep these activities a joy of the season, is an organizer for occasions and their preparations. Encourage your family to help you keep the list as current as possible, thus allowing you to combine errands and avoid unnecessary trips—or decorating cupcakes in your new party dress.

Occasion	Family Member Attending	Date and Time	Transportation	Food to Take	Gift to Take

Christmas Card List

Names	rec'd	sent	Names	rec'd	sent

127

Sunday, November 1

Monday, November 2

Tuesday, November 3

Wednesday, November 4

Thursday, November 5

Friday, November 6

Saturday, November 7

Sunday, November 8

Monday, November 9

Tuesday, November 10

Wednesday, November 11

Thursday, November 12

Friday, November 13

Saturday, November 14

Sunday, November 15

Monday, November 16

Tuesday, November 17

Wednesday, November 18

Thursday, November 19

Friday, November 20

Saturday, November 21

Sunday, November 22

Monday, November 23

Tuesday, November 24

Wednesday, November 25

Thursday, November 26   *Thanksgiving*

Friday, November 27

Saturday, November 28

Sunday, November 29

Monday, November 30

Tuesday, December 1

Wednesday, December 2

Thursday, December 3

Friday, December 4

Saturday, December 5

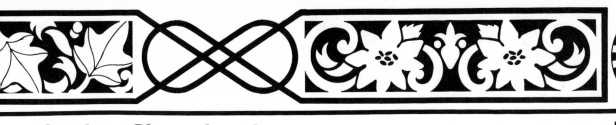

Sunday, December 6

Monday, December 7

Tuesday, December 8

Wednesday, December 9

Thursday, December 10

Friday, December 11

Saturday, December 12

Sunday, December 13

___

Monday, December 14

___

Tuesday, December 15

___

Wednesday, December 16

___

Thursday, December 17

___

Friday, December 18

___

Saturday, December 19

Sunday, December 20

Monday, December 21

Tuesday, December 22

Wednesday, December 23

Thursday, December 24

Friday, December 25   Christmas

Saturday, December 26

Sunday, December 27

Monday, December 28

Tuesday, December 29

Wednesday, December 30

Thursday, December 31

Friday, January 1   New Year's Day

Saturday, January 2

Holiday Snapshots

Contributors

Design: Carol Middleton
Editorial Assistance: Shelley Ticheli, Rebecca
   Gilliland
Cover photograph: Charles Walton
Art: Cindia Pickering, Steve Logan, Don Smith
Production: Jerry Higdon

Special thanks to the following people at *Southern Living* for their expert advice and time: Shelley Ticheli, Jean Wickstrom Liles, Susan Payne, Karen Lingo, Dixie Snell, John Floyd, and Bruce Roberts.

Designers

Dorinda Beaumont, gold crocheted ornaments 38.

Alexandra Eames, coffee can planter 51, felt picture frames 52.

John Floyd, fruit & berry tree 34.

Edith Gasci, animal dolls 47.

Merri Gow, wine bags 54.

Kathryn Green, cross-stitched lids 41.

Charlotte Hagood, fabric boxes 56.

Julia Hamilton, holly kitchen wreath 15, hurricane globes 19, Christmas seals 55.

Mary Higbee, tissue paper gift sacks 53.

Norman K. Johnson, selecting the right tree 27.

Jan Kirkpatrick, shell collector's tree 30-31.

Karen Lingo, cranberry wreath 16.

Ellen McCarn, gingerbread family 88.

Rose Mooney, jewels for the tree 38.

Sunny O'Neil, nut basket 23, Queen Anne's lace ornaments 26.

Sue Unruh Pack, pearl-beaded snowflakes 40.

Katherine Pearson, gourmet collections 109, tool kits 109.

Kay Pendley, nut & pine cone wreath 18.

Shelley Ticheli, ribbons on pillows 20, ribbon on mirror 20, spice ornaments 32, walnut ornaments 32, festive linens 36.

Bill Whisenant, Norfolk Island pine 21.

Judy Williams, appliquéd stockings 44.

Photographers

Bruce Roberts, 4, top left 20, 50, 115, 119, 120, 121.

Bob Lancaster, top left 22, top right 25, bottom left 26, 55, 108, color photographs 109.

Geoffrey Gilbert, 122.

Mike Clemmer, bottom 8, 19, top right 22, 23, 106, 107, 117, 118.

Van Chaplin, 7, top left and right 8, top left and right 15, 24, bottom 25.

Mac Jamieson, bottom right 22, 88-90, 101-106.

Beth Maynor, top left and right 21, top right 26, 27.

Sylvia Martin, 44, 53.

John O'Hagan, 16, bottom left 21, 34, 40, 41, 47, 56, 116.

Charles E. Walton, 3, 18, top and bottom 20, bottom left 22, 30-33, 35, 38, 59, 99, 113, 123.

Louis Joyner, bottom 6, 9, 17, top left 26, black & white photographs 109.

Taylor Lewis, 61.

Jerome Drown, insert title page, 66, 77, 82, 85, 97.

Kent Kirkley, 68.

David Nance, 5.

©Peter M. Fine 1978, 39, 51, 52.